BFI Film Classics

The BFI Film Classics series introduces, interprets and celebrates
landmarks of world cinema. Each volume offers an argument for
the film's 'classic' status, together with discussion of its production
and reception history, its place within a genre or national cinema, an
account of its technical and aesthetic importance, and in many cases,
the author's personal response to the film.

For a full list of titles in the series, please visit
https://www.bloomsbury.com/uk/series/bfi-film-classics/

Rosemary's Baby

Michael Newton

THE BRITISH FILM INSTITUTE
Bloomsbury Publishing Plc
50 Bedford Square, London, WC1B 3DP, UK
1385 Broadway, New York, NY 10018, USA

BLOOMSBURY is a trademark of Bloomsbury Publishing Plc

First published in Great Britain 2020 by Bloomsbury on behalf of the
British Film Institute
21 Stephen Street, London W1T 1LN
www.bfi.org.uk

The BFI is the lead organisation for film in the UK and the distributor of Lottery funds for film.
Our mission is to ensure that film is central to our cultural life, in particular by supporting and
nurturing the next generation of filmmakers and audiences. We serve a public role which covers
the cultural, creative and economic aspects of film in the UK.

Cover artwork: Mark Swan
Series cover design: Louise Dugdale
Series text design: ketchup/SE14
Images from *Rosemary's Baby* © 1968 Paramount
Pictures Corporation and William Castle Enterprises Inc.

A catalogue record for this book is available from the British Library.

A catalog record for this book is available from the Library of Congress.

ISBN: PB: 978-1-8445-7952-5
        ePDF: 978-1-8387-1901-2
        ePUB: 978-1-8445-7954-9

Series: BFI Film Classics

Typeset by Integra Software Services Pvt. Ltd
Printed and bound in India

To find out more about our authors and books visit www.bloomsbury.com
and sign up for our newsletters.

Contents

Acknowledgements

I first heard about *Rosemary's Baby* as a seven-year-old child in the early 1970s, through the warning words of a cartoon evangelical tract. I was supposed to sequester this pamphlet in a public place and so, it was anticipated, save the soul of whoever would providentially find it. There the film was designated as a dark beguilement, one of many counter-cultural attempts to ridicule religion. That tract left me with an uneasy feeling about the movie. Though I admire Polanski's film enormously, and have grown to feel a passion for his work, that unease has never quite departed. For me, writing on the film taps into deep anxieties and touches troubled beliefs. When it comes to exploring this movie, this may be a useful burden. It has never seemed a film like other films to me but has long struck me as something set apart, taboo, and strange. Writing about it has left that sense unexorcized.

Given the distinguished company of other authors, to write a book in this series also has seemed to me something set apart. I thank Victoria Hobbs at A. M. Heath for speaking on my behalf; Jenna Steventon and Clarissa Sutherland at Palgrave for their help and for this second opportunity to write on a film classic; and the excellent Rebecca Barden at Bloomsbury for seeing it to the finish. I much appreciate the work done on this book by the team at Bloomsbury, especially by Rebecca Willford, Katherine Bosiacki, Ken Bruce, and Sophia Contento. I am grateful to the efficient, knowledgeable and helpful library staff at the BFI Library on the South Bank. I thank Roger Luckhurst for his useful advice, and Evert Jan van Leeuwen for his friendship and Gothic knowledge. Over the last twenty-five years, I have discussed *Rosemary's Baby* with students at UCL, Central Saint Martins College and Leiden University. It would be a hard task to disentangle all I learnt from them from what I imagine to be my own ideas about the film, but in this regard I am particularly indebted to Eddie d'Oliveira and Mark Broughton. Part of the material here draws on an article on conspiracy film I wrote for *The Guardian*, and I am grateful to Paul Laity and Nicholas Wroe for their encouragement and support. I especially thank Lena Müller, whose kindness, support and affection made the writing of this book possible. I dedicate my work on this book to Karl Miller, with whom I first read James Hogg's devilish *Confessions*, and who, I believe, was doubly my teacher and a friend.

An Initiation

Rosemary's Baby enacts the closing of a trap. It ensnares Rosemary and it ensnares you. While comedy gifts us with the sense that we may extricate ourselves from every bad situation, in tragedy no-one escapes. The terrible efficiency of Polanski's film consists in its closing off all possibilities for rescue. In Gothic, in the conspiracy film, we enjoy representations of our powerlessness, we appreciate the elegant inescapability of the traps we're in. In what Polanski has declared to be his favourite moment in the film, Rosemary reclines on a chaise-longue in Dr Hill's office; against all odds, she believes she has found refuge. Protected, understood, she allows herself to relax and dream of motherhood, a golden reverie of happy families and contentment. She wakes, and Dr Hill, her protector, softly enters the room, and then, a few seconds behind him, creep in the physician and the skulking husband whom she believes have organized her rape, controlled her body, and plotted to abduct and likely kill her yet unborn child. The moment erases hope; her saviour proves complicit with her adversaries. Much of the power of Polanski's movie finds expression in that moment, its brightly lit refusal to soothe or succour.

Rosemary's Baby is one of the greatest late 1960s films and one of the best of all horror movies, an outstanding modern Gothic tale. An art-house fable and an elegant popular entertainment, it finds its home on the cusp between a cinema of sentiment and one of sensation. In its structure, a European absurdist sensibility comes to the puritan ground of America. The film updates the witch from archetypal terror to the exemplar of our contemporary fear of domination. It's an atypical horror film, one that foregoes shocks in favour of atmosphere and anxiety, a slow, edgy story fabricated by a man filled with natural exuberance; gusto pulses beneath its restrained menace.

In horror, it's the idea and not the size of the chainsaw that provokes fear. Terror comes with imagination and imaginative involvement in the endangerment of others. *Rosemary's Baby* provides a fairy tale for adults; it preys on adult fears, especially our fear of being infantilized. It explores the plight of the married, the paranoia of the mother-to-be. In the pressbook for the movie, one of its stars, John Cassavetes declared that the movie 'is the most violent, non-violent picture I've ever worked in. It reeks of mystery, horror and eeriness, with never a blow being struck.'

Gothic frequently depends upon the victimization of a woman, while customarily it is the woman who proves the survivor. In horror, the victim must rescue themselves, the oppressed must become her own liberator. *Rosemary's Baby* relies on all these generic facts and subverts them. It is the epitome of the genre it dismantles. In 1968, at the counterculture's high-point, *Rosemary's Baby* examines the violence that unknits the social or that perhaps really *is* the social. It stands as a shining example of something contrary to the sheen of 1960s modern life.

I have divided the book that follows into three parts: 'The pledge', that sets out the making of the film; 'The turn', that explores its meanings and resonances; and a flourish of 'The prestige', that examines its reception and cultural impact. Throughout, my reading of the film depends on three interrelated ideas: first, that the film presents itself as just a film, a work of art bound up in the paradoxes of performance; second, that the movie dramatizes a theatre of relations based on power, constraint and the loss of the individual will; and third, that the movie melds many of the themes and fashions of the late 1960s. It both floats in a sea of context and explodes the very idea of context, given its involvement in a system of meaning based on connection, coincidence and conspiracy.

1 The Pledge

Hollywood in crisis?

In 1959, John Cassavetes wrote an article explaining 'What's Wrong With Hollywood'; it began, 'Hollywood is not failing. It has failed.'[1] In the early 1960s, the public, the critics, the film-makers themselves felt the movie business to be a moribund concern. *Rosemary's Baby* emerged at a moment that saw a breaking up of the Hollywood consensus around censorship, as movies broke taboos, permitted swearing, were increasingly frank in their depiction of sex and violence, and were ready to forego or subvert the standing traditions of narrative coherence. As Polanski put it in an interview, it was the demise of 'the Hitchcock audience'.[2] 1967 saw the release of *The Fox*, *Point Blank*, *Bonnie and Clyde*, all films that were in some regard provocations in a war between conservative values and progressive art. Film-makers defended the new frankness; asked about the violence in his movies, Polanski pointed to its prevalence in real life. The disputes over *Bonnie and Clyde* showed that films could become battlegrounds, pitched between those who were 'hip' to it and those who were not.

Many deplored cinematic violence and explicit sex. In September 1967, Jack Valenti, president of the Motion Pictures Association of America, worried about some in the young audience 'of a psychedelic breed, hunkered up over pot and acid, and lurching off on supranatural romps and trips'.[3] In 1967, President Lyndon B. Johnson ordered a National Commission on Obscenity and Pornography, designed to investigate the loosening of standards. In the fall of 1969, a new group, 'A Pledge of Conscience', declared their intention to censor and prevent violence in scripts. Yet pressure for greater censorship was parried by calls for Hollywood to take up the maturity and urgency of European film. Late in 1968, the Motion

Picture Association of America brought in a ratings system, designed to sidestep direct censorship and palliate fears about content.

This new spirit in cinema took hold after a period of decline for the American movie business. The number of films released went down – from 332 in 1952 to a mere 143 in 1963, the low-point in terms of Hollywood production. The number of cinemas dwindled, from around 18 000 at the end of the Second World War to about 12 000 in 1962 (though there were also 5 000 new drive-in cinemas). There were certainly fewer films, but those few that did become hits made more money: from 1895 to 1960, only twenty films grossed more than $10 million, between 1960 and 1969, sixty films did. As young producer Robert Evans would realize, TV had ushered in the end of habitual film-going; the cinema trip was now an event.

The movies that Hollywood did make looked tired, products of 'daddy's cinema' with a style and set of interests squarely set against those of the American young. From the late 1950s into the 1960s the average age of the cinema audience steadily rose. A youth market had emerged that was unimpressed by mainstream films. In part, the new violence and the new sexual frankness were motivated by a desire to boost the box office receipts: sex and violence was something that television did not (yet) do. Cinema positioned itself as the adult alternative to TV. In another sense, the explicitness was also doctrinal, an ideologically motivated candour. All the arts were busy freeing themselves of censorship and restraint.

Rosemary's Baby, therefore, saw the light in a world caught up in a moment of cultural hesitation, a shift in values and understanding. Vitally, this confusion seeps into the movie itself, radically destabilizing its sense of what witches are. On one level, through Rosemary herself and her writer friend, Hutch, it clings to the ancient belief that witches are evil, perverse doers of harm through magic. The witches themselves tap into an increasingly popular twentieth-century reading in which they see themselves as victims of a life-denying religion. Most modern of all is the perspective taken by Guy, Rosemary's husband, for whom witchcraft hardly matters one way or another, simply being a neat, and morally indifferent, way to attain your desires.

A look back at Ira Levin

Before anything else, *Rosemary's Baby* was Ira Levin's creation, the work of one of the most successful post-war American writers of popular fiction. He's best remembered as the author of a mere seven highly successful novels, many of which went on to be adapted for film, most notably: *A Kiss Before Dying* (1953) (filmed in 1956 and again in 1991); *Rosemary's Baby* (1967); *The Stepford Wives* (1972) (filmed in 1975 and 2004); *The Boys From Brazil* (1976) (filmed in 1978); and *Sliver* (1991) (filmed in 1993). Levin was the poet laureate of paranoia, a man dedicated to the dismantling of the apparent world to expose the plots beneath. Like Rosemary, the mechanized brides of Stepford and the Hitler clones of *The Boys From Brazil* were icons of a period tainted by Lee Harvey Oswald, Watergate and the Pentagon Papers. The truth was out there, concealed but discoverable, horrifying in its very certainty. For Levin, in his 1967 novel, Rosemary was the victim of a plot, a genuine sacrifice to a dark intrigue. His story would tap too into the 1960s sense of confusion over marriage and the life of the American housewife. These vogueish concerns were meant to catch on; this was a book reputedly designed to be a bestseller.[4] It succeeded in its aim: by June 1968, it had sold 2.3 million copies.[5] Even before the book was in print, the rights had already been sold to a movie producer, and the first step towards turning Levin's tale into a movie had been taken.

The tingler

In the mid-1970s, talking to a psychiatrist at a dinner party, William Castle, *Rosemary's Baby's* producer, assured the man that he had no deeply hidden fears. Privately, he thought: 'But I knew otherwise. My life had been built on fear.'[6] Castle, *né* Schloss, a huckster of schlock horror, hardly looked the type to be afraid; Polanski described him as 'a red-faced giant of a man with a thatch of close-cropped white hair

Lauren Bacall on set with William Castle; Castle's presence outside the phone booth as Rosemary is on the run.

and a cigar permanently clamped between his teeth'.[7] Yet fear, and the evocation of fear, had indeed been his life. One of his earliest memories was wetting himself with fright during a visit with his dad to the horror play, *The Monster*.[8] His mum died when he was ten, his dad (of a coronary) when he was eleven, and so he went to live with his much older sister in New York. There he became a stage-door Johnny, befriending Bela Lugosi and acting as stage manager to the touring play of *Dracula*. At the age of twenty-five, he inherited $10 000 from his dad and from then on, pursued a career that melded together creaky artistic endeavour with a showman's flair for advertising.

Castle was the king of the gimmick, with a hidden desire to win an Oscar. With one eye on the art of Welles and Hitchcock, he approached cinema in the beguiling spirit of ardency and vividness, linking back to vaudeville and the fairground. His life depended on the sparking of reactions in a room of strangers. He became famous for a series of carnivalesque horror flicks, each of them publicized by some novel promotional stunt. Not unjustly, Polanski saw Castle's films as 'plutôt minables' (rather shabby).[9] Yet the formula hit the spot: according to Castle, his movie *Macabre* (1958) cost $90 000 to make, and made $5 million; in 1968, The William Castle Fan Club had 150 000 members.[10]

Castle dealt in a weirdly immersive cinema experience, with gizmos and tricks that took the film beyond the screen, some given their own brand-name: skeletons flew over the audience ('Emergo'); a chair sparked electric shocks for *The Tingler* (1959) ('Percepto'); seats shook; people were hired to scream or 'faint'; a 'Coward's Corner' was built for *Homicidal* (1961), for those who, after a 'Fright Break', claimed their cash back on the basis of being too scared to watch to the end.[11] The audiences for *Macabre* signed insurance policies against death by fright. All this manifested Castle's own response to Hollywood's falling audiences; like widescreen or 3-D, these gambits were a reason still to see films in the cinema, keeping it a 'theatrical' experience.

In 1967, Castle believed that the 'bottom had fallen out of the horror films'.[12] It was then that he received the galley proofs for a new novel – Levin's *Rosemary's Baby*. Castle understood that Hitchcock had been the first to read the galleys but had passed on the movie.[13] Whether this was true or not, Castle immediately saw the story's potential. Levin's agent, Marvin Birdt, offered the film rights for $100 000, with another $50 000, if the book became a bestseller – and 5 per cent of the net profits. The deal was struck, but Castle was now left wondering how he'd raise the money. It was then that he heard from Bob Evans at Paramount.

The kid who stayed in the picture

Robert Evans was the man who brought *Rosemary's Baby* together, the third fount of charisma, with Castle and Polanski, who would turn Levin's novel into the great movie it would become. He was born Robert J. Shapers in New York in 1930, the son of a Harlem dentist. Young Evans ran a company making women's slacks. He had been a child actor on the radio, but Hollywood must have seemed far off, until he was spotted, looking handsome, by Norma Shearer at a swimming pool, and was cast as her former husband, Irving Thalberg, in *The Man With A Thousand Faces* (1957). Soon after, Evans was discovered, again, this time by Darryl Zanuck in a New York nightclub, and picked to play a Spanish bullfighter opposite Ava Gardner in *The Sun Also Rises* (1957).

In Zanuck's authority, Evans glimpsed the person he wanted to be, the work he wanted to do: he would remake himself as a studio executive and producer. He set about this task with customary verve. A piece by Peter Bart hyping him in *The New York Times* brought him to the attention of Charles Bluhdorn. The founder and chairman of Gulf & Western, Bluhdorn was an auto-parts tycoon who in 1966 had acquired majority stock at Paramount. This was the first buy-out of a major studio by a company outside the entertainment industry. Though mocked as an ignorant outsider to the business, Bluhdorn would prove a hands-on owner, eager to get involved. One quick way of stamping his authority on things was to replace the middle-aged Howard Koch, Paramount's head of film production, with young Evans.

Evans's appointment was part of a first wave of replacements of ageing studio bosses by the young: Evans was in his mid-thirties; at Fox, Richard Zanuck was thirty-four; and David Picker at United Artists was thirty-six. On the other hand, when Evans was appointed, Adolph Zukor, Paramount's chairman emeritus, was ninety-six years old.

There were many who were sceptical of Evans's ability to make a success of the failing Paramount Studios. He was soon nicknamed 'Bluhdorn's Folly' (or, in Jack Rosenstein's quip, 'Bluhdorn's Blowjob'). He needed a calling card film, a genuine hit that would secure his position at Paramount and help reverse the studio's run of bad luck. He had the rights to *The Detective* (1968) in hand, and then began with two Neil Simon comedies, *Barefoot in the Park* (1967) and *The Odd Couple* (1968). Both were hits, but lacked the culture-defining power of the genuinely big movie. The property was the star and, hearing from Castle, Evans knew that *Rosemary's Baby* was the star property to make his career.

The deal

Castle came to Evans with the proposal; the young executive scented success. Bernard Donnenfeld, Evans's business partner, arranged a meeting between Castle and Charles Bluhdorn. Castle wanted financial backing, but he also wanted to direct. That was never an option, and as Evans tells it, he bullied Castle into merely producing.[14] While they arranged the deal with Castle, Evans already had Roman Polanski in his sights.

Impressed by Polanksi's *Repulsion* (1965) and seeing its kinship to Levin's fantasy, Evans enticed the young director to Los Angeles. He knew Polanski loved skiing and offered him a Robert Redford property, called *Downhill Racer*, or *Ski Bum*. And then, as Polanski describes it: 'he gave me the skiing script, and said "I also have something else I would like you to read". He put a bunch of book galleys on the desk, these long strips of yellowish paper, and said "read this first". I went to the Beverly Hills Hotel, and just out of curiosity I started to read it.'[15] Jetlagged as he was, he started on the page proofs at midnight, almost dismissed it as a Doris Day movie, and then as he read on, was hooked; at four o'clock, he was still reading. The morning after Polanski finished the novel, he met Evans at the studio and said yes.[16]

Evans's style, youth and good-looks impressed Polanksi. But for now, Castle was singularly unimpressed by the prospect of a hip, Polish art-house director taking over his baby. An interview was set up. Put off at first by what he perceived to be Polanski's vanity, Castle was quickly won over. On three vital points he and Polanski were in complete agreement: the film should follow the book as closely as possible; they should let the actors act; and telling the story was hugely more important than 'arty' shots.

The project was agreed. In giving the film to Polanski, one of the most talented directors of the decade, and someone working at the very height of his powers, it seemed that *Rosemary's Baby* could be everything that Evans needed it to be.

Roman by Polanski

In 1984, Polanski began an interview with London's *Time Out*, by declaring, '"Look ... Let's get one thing clear before we start ... I am *not* an asshole, OK?".'[17] That pre-emptive act of self-description felt necessary to a man who for fifteen years had been a suspect figure to the world's press and for much of his public. Yet hostility to Polanski had always been there, often manifesting itself in insulting comments on his shortness and his looks. In 1969, *The Times* suggested he was a 'merry' man resembling Beatrix Potter's town mouse; in his *Biographical Dictionary of Film*, David Thomson remarks that 'the tiny, rather ugly man had asserted himself'.[18] In 1986 in an interview, he expressed his sense of persecution: 'I get the feeling people hate me and that I've got so many enemies I need to get out of town as soon as possible.'[19] Polanski is one of the few people for whom such expressions seem more than paranoia.

Roman Polanski, pensive, during the shooting of *Repulsion* (1965).

When he made *Rosemary's Baby*, Polanski could have been seen as being as much of a horror film director as Castle, someone perhaps likely to be pinned down in a genre. Of course, Polanski's career would not play out like that at all, and over fifty years he would prove one of the most versatile writer-directors to work in cinema, a person experimenting with genres and turning them inside out.

On 18 August 1933, Raymond Polanski, the son of a Polish Jewish family, was born in Paris; while still a young child, the family moved back to Kraków; the Nazi invasion trapped the family there. His mother was resourceful, resilient, a beautiful woman who in social terms married beneath her. His earliest memories are of a childhood passed in the war, walled in by the ghetto, watching German propaganda films being broadcast in Padgorze Square, peering through the barbed wire. On 13 March 1943, alone among his family he escaped the liquidation of the Kraków ghetto, and went to live on the land with a Catholic farming family, only returning to Kraków as the Russians rolled in. Only after the war did Roman discover that his mother had been killed in Auschwitz. It would be impossible to say how deeply such terrible experiences have determined Polanski's life and character, his vision of the world. Maria Kornatowska has plausibly argued that 'all of Polanski's films ... have been about the war, and ... the simultaneous combination of claustrophobia and agoraphobia which so characterised the ghetto experience'.[20]

Young Roman began to try acting, and ended up as a young actor on *The Merry Gang* (*Wesoła gromadka*), a children's radio show; soon he was appearing in films. Expelled from the Kraków art school, and desperately attempting to avoid the draft, he found a role in Andrzej Wajda's *A Generation* (*Pokolenie*) (1955). Polanski's acting career was typified by taking on the part of young roughs; he became an expert in the role of hoodlum, playing against his smallness, his youthful appearance, expressing his capacity to look simultaneously innocent and wicked.

Polanski's life was finally set in the right direction by his finding a place at the film school in Lodz, one of eight students for the directors' course that year. Here Polanski was 'bowled over' by *Citizen Kane*, *Rashomon* and *Los Olvidados*. On *Rashomon*, as with *Kane*, he was struck by the notion that 'the relativity of truth, seen through the eyes of three different characters, was made for the cinema. No other medium could have done it so well.'[21] This lesson would, in time, play out in *Rosemary's Baby* too.

A penchant for mayhem animates all his student shorts; *Murder* (*Morderstwo*) and *The Smile* (*Usmiech zebiczny*) (both 1957) channel a Hitchcockian interest in violence and voyeurism. After a trip to Paris he returned to Lodz and made a short, *Breaking Up the Party*, and an absurdist allegory, *Two Men and a Wardrobe* (1957). The latter was designed to win a prize and promptly won one, a Bronze Medal from Brussels.

Soon after this, he met and fell in love with Barbara Kwiatkowski, a young actor who appeared in his excellent diploma piece, *When Angels Fall* (*Gdy spadaja anioly*) (1959), a romantic, compassionate film about an old lavatory attendant's epiphany. The couple married in September 1959. With Jerzy Skolimowski, he now wrote his first feature-length script for *Knife in the Water* (*Nóz w wodzie*), before going to Paris with his new wife. He returned to Poland to make *Mammals* (*Ssaki*), financed by Wojciech Frykowski (who would later be murdered alongside Sharon Tate), and to direct *Knife in the Water* (both 1962). Around this time, he separated from his wife, who was having an affair with the movie-director Gillo Pontecorvo. *Knife in the Water* was a highly confident debut, a dark tale of male rivalries, whose well-heeled, yacht-owning sports journalist character and his placid, watchful wife seemed very far from the world of social realism. Inevitably Wladyslaw Gomulka, head of the Communist Party, maligned the movie.

Facing such opposition, Polanski's career might have stalled. However, back in Paris, Polanski met Gérard Brach, the writer with whom he would collaborate on nine completed movies. Together the

Catherine Deneuve with Polanski, filming *Repulsion* in London; Polanski with Donald Pleasance on location in Lindisfarne while filming *Cul-de-Sac* (1966).

two men started writing the movie that would become *Cul-de-Sac*
(1966). And then Polanski's fortunes changed. *Mammals* won a prize
at Tours and, more vitally, *Knife in the Water* won the Critics Prize
at Venice and was nominated for an Oscar (only losing, honourably,
to Fellini's *Otto e Mezzo*). The possibility to direct a new movie
arose, one produced by a Pole living in London; together with Brach,
Polanski wrote *Repulsion* in seventeen days.

To make *Repulsion*, Polanski moved to London. Starring
Catherine Deneuve as the benumbed Carole, the film follows the
heroine's murderous breakdown in South Kensington. Polanski's
charisma and vitality won him many friends, and he became quickly
a fixture on the swinging scene. He met Warren Beatty, hung out
at the Playboy Club and the Ad Lib, schmoozed with the Beatles.
Meanwhile, in what would become a typical problem, Polanski's
meticulous work on *Repulsion* sent the production over-budget
and over schedule. However, Polanski's care paid off; it remains
a magnificent and intense movie. The film won the Silver Bear at
Berlin; the money-men were delighted, and funded Polanski and
Brach's pet project, *Cul-de-Sac*. This would be a film about 'freedom
of expression', about just setting up a situation, starting a story, and
seeing what happens.[22] It failed to reproduce *Repulsion's* success, but
despite that it stands as one of Polanski's finest films.

Helped by the sharkish American producer, Martin Ransohoff,
Polanski now made a comedy-horror film, *The Fearless Vampire
Killers* (1967), an anarchic, playful romp, closer to *Carry on
Screaming* than *Dracula*, and, for this viewer at least, a pleasure from
beginning to end. Polanski acted in it too, looking boyish and sweetly
bewildered. Playing opposite him was a young, highly beautiful, good-
natured Texan actress, Sharon Tate. It was Ransohoff's idea that the
role should go to Sharon Tate; at first, Polanski was rather against her.
Yet the two of them were quickly attracted to each other, even though
Tate was still officially with her hairdresser boyfriend, Jay Sebring.
Polanski and Tate took LSD together, an experience that would feed
into *Rosemary's Baby*. Meanwhile the deal with Ransohoff was

souring, as the producer started butchering and remoulding Polanski's film. It was at this stage, just as he and Sharon were pairing up, that Polanski heard from Bob Evans and flew to Hollywood.

In a life marked by experiences more terrible than most of us can contemplate, Polanski grew up in make-believe – in play, in art, in cinema. One key to understanding him and his movies is his immersion in art, his strong desire to fabricate imaginary worlds; his power (as a person and as a director) is to make those dreams come to life. He disbelieves the doctrine of 'the auteur', and yet his films emphatically realize a personal vision, projecting on screen what is in his head.[23] In the 1960s, and perhaps later, he was a man untroubled by humility. His self-belief then appears inexhaustible; given the quality of his work, it also seems justified.

The script

Having agreed not only to direct the film but also to write the script, Polanski flew back to London for three months to work on it. On this occasion, he worked alone. He 'reread the book – the magic still held – pencilled out the irrelevant passages, and dictated a preliminary draft to Concepta, our Cadre Films secretary'.[24] The first draft was 260–270 pages long. Cuts were made. Work went fast, and the finished version, for William Castle Enterprises, dated 24 July 1967, weighs in at 167 pages.

Polanski did not really draw shots in advance or storyboard the film, yet it's all there in the written text. In composing it, he stuck closely to the novel but did not particularly collaborate with Levin; they spoke on the phone but only met later. Levin remembered it this way: 'He called me several times, which was very un-Hollywood. His questions were never general, only specific – for instance, Roman wanted to know which issue of *The New Yorker* Guy was reading when he saw the ad for the shirt. I didn't know the answer.'[25] Levin is far from a great stylist, but he's certainly a skilled and effective writer. The book is one already adapted to a cinematic eye, and so it was that when the film's script came to be written, Polanski would scrupulously shadow the original text. As the review in *The Times* put it: 'Polanski has settled to follow the book line by line, move by move. Every phrase, every description of an expression or gesture is followed precisely.'[26] For Kenneth Tynan (later a collaborator with Polanski on the script of *Macbeth*), 'There has seldom been a clearer demonstration that the director is not always the principal creator of a film.' Though he goes on to add, 'Levin is the creator, and Polanski the artist.'[27]

The moonchild

When it came to casting, it was clear that the film would stand or fall with whoever acted Rosemary. Polanski believed Tuesday Weld should play the part; he'd already wanted her for *Fearless Vampire Killers* and, moreover, she was a friend of Sharon Tate's.[28] Blonde, all-American, a sturdy five foot four, Weld matched Levin's image of Rosemary as resembling the voluptuous red-haired movie star Piper Laurie (or, as he puts it, Laurie Piper). This putative confidently sexy, worldly wise Rosemary would never reach the screen. For both Castle and Evans already wanted Mia Farrow. Bob Evans mentioned Farrow, and Polanski watched her act in some *Peyton Place* episodes. Soon after Polanski and Farrow met at a nightclub called The Daisy. The director was impressed.

The daughter of movie director John Farrow and movie star Maureen O'Sullivan (of the *Tarzan* movies and *The Thin Man* [1934] fame), Farrow grew up in a semi-detached relationship to the movie world, both immersed and somehow apart. Her godmother was Louella Parsons, and George Cukor was her godfather; her first crush, Michael Boyer, was Charles Boyer's son; her first drink (a brandy Alexander) was bought for her by Brendan Behan.

These connections to celebrity and stardom were off-set by a family ethos that rather looked down on the show-business world. John Farrow felt himself, not without reason, to be out of place in Hollywood circles, being an earnest writer and a devout, if morally wayward Catholic; his hagiography, *Damien the Leper* became a religious classic; unusually for a resident of Tinseltown, he was made a Papal Knight. Born on 9 February 1945, Mia (Maria de Lourdes Villiers) Farrow had two older brothers, Michael and Joseph, and would have four younger siblings. In 1954, aged nine, the scrawny Mia contracted polio, was packed off to an isolation ward and then consigned to a lengthy childhood convalescence. A convent education in England fostered a life of schoolgirl dramas and schoolgirl piety.

In 1958, aged nineteen, her brother Michael died in a plane crash. The huge shock of it stunned the family. In 1963, as catastrophic for young Mia was her father's death from a heart attack. Farrow certainly idealized her father, seeing in him an exemplar of probity and virtue, rather unlike the louche character perceived by his contemporaries.[29] Around this time, Farrow was setting out to be an actress. In 1963, playing Cecily in *The Importance of Being Earnest* on Broadway at the Madison Avenue Playhouse, she was spotted and taken up by Jack Merrivale and Vivien Leigh. Leigh recommended her to 20th Century Fox; despite some wariness about the long-term commitment involved, she joined the cast of the upcoming TV soap opera, *Peyton Place* (1964–1969). The movie version of *Peyton Place* (1957) had been Fox's biggest earner so far, and they were impatient to capitalize on the success. When the series first aired in the fall of 1964, the sex symbol was meant to be brunette Barbara Parkins but instead viewers fell for Farrow. By October 1965, *Peyton Place* was sixth in the Nielsen ratings.

In October 1964, Farrow met Frank Sinatra on the Fox lot. An unlikely romance developed, one in which, perhaps, Farrow made the running. He was forty-eight, she was nineteen years old. Entering into a relationship with him, she was suddenly an incongruous part of a generation of ageing stars, her mother's and father's generation. In August 1965, when Farrow and Sinatra took a cruise on the *Southern Breeze*, Claudette Colbert, Merle Oberon and Rosalind Russell were unofficial chaperones.

Meanwhile, Sinatra was occupied trying to find a place for himself in the mid-1960s music market, one increasingly dominated by youth. The age-gap between himself and Farrow quickly became the subject of jokes; Jackie Mason's gags about their bed-time routine ('Frank soaks his dentures, Mia brushes her braces') led to shots being fired at the comic's hotel room. Journalists saw Mia Farrow as a proto-flower-child whimsically choosing an older man.

During a decade when repudiation of the older generation was normative, Farrow fashioned her own image as one of embracement: 'I haven't been in touch with my own generation much. Most of my friends have been older people, like Salvador Dali.'[30] He was positioning himself in awkward, disturbing ways in relation to the younger generation; recording on 1 February 1967, the sweetly incestuous song, 'Something Stupid', a love-duet with his daughter, Nancy Sinatra, only deepened the indignity. Farrow would be some years younger than her step-children. Ava Gardner once remarked to her that she 'was the child she and Frank never had'.[31]

Farrow certainly seemed to appreciate father-figures; there was Dali, and she actually called Yul Brynner, 'Dad'. Much later, she could confess that Sinatra's after-shave reminded her of her father: 'I can say it now, they had the same identical smell.'[32]

Mia Farrow painting her hut on the set of *Rosemary's Baby*.

Farrow was childlike, flapperesque, closer to Twiggy than Marilyn Monroe. For some, Farrow was too fey, too thin, too much a gawky, half-grown-up girl, and too little of a tough woman. In the early 1970s, clearly thinking of *Rosemary's Baby*, Molly Haskell imagined Farrow as one of the 1960s numerous Lolita-women, a nubile descendant of Shirley Temple, and a will-less somnambulist (so long a central figure in Gothic), someone 'whose very passivity allows her to become an agent of evil'.[33] Pauline Kael shared in this queasy ambivalence, putting her down as 'adorable in a beautiful little sick-kitten way', a 'little rabbit looking for a hutch'.[34] Farrow sometimes presented herself in similar ways, someone defined by fears and otherworldliness.

Farrow could appear intangible and elusive, 'an icon of contemporary mutability itself'.[35] '"I'm like a kaleidoscope ... I see a different person every time I look in a mirror",' she declared.[36] She was, above all, young, only twenty-two when she played Rosemary, younger than Jim Morrison or Janis Joplin. She was both star and anti-star, part of a generation of actors who stood out for freedom, for all they captured the heights of fame. Her obvious ability to grab worldly success, a necessary touch of steel in her, militates against these readings of her as intangibly frail.

She and Sinatra married on 29 July 1966. They planned to shoot *The Detective*, Bob Evans's property, for Fox. Just then the script for *Rosemary's Baby* was sent to her. Sinatra read it in bed one night, and remarked that he couldn't see Farrow in the part. She couldn't see herself in the part either, but accepted it anyway.[37] Farrow's decision to play Rosemary was an ambitious one. Given Sinatra's hostility to her having an independent career, perhaps it was inevitable that her decision should put strain on the marriage.[38]

With its own concerns about youth's relationship to age, her 'real-life' marriage to Sinatra is and is not present in *Rosemary's Baby*. More than most actors, her personal life has been felt to play out in her on-screen roles, and she has seemed someone defined by her parents, her lovers. In her then partner, Woody Allen's *Hannah and Her Sisters* (1986), Maureen O'Sullivan plays Farrow's on-screen mum. Mia Farrow and Rosemary are distinct, but in ways typical of the film they are also entwined, one incarnating the other.

I suppose all actors are selfish and vain

Everyone would in time agree that Farrow was pretty much perfect as Rosemary; when it came to casting her husband, Guy Woodhouse, opinions would be more divided.

Fresh from playing opposite Farrow in the spy-thriller, *A Dandy In Aspic* (1968), the British star Laurence Harvey lobbied to play Guy; Polanski also considered the blond, handsome and well-connected photographer Peter Beard. Neither was right. Warren Beatty turned the role down, as not important enough. Jack Nicholson tried out for the part but would have been too rakish and sinister. The first choice, however, for both Evans and Polanski was always Robert Redford. However, Paramount were suing Redford for walking out of a western movie called *Blue*, so he was sadly out of the question. Redford and Polanski met to discuss the film at Oblaths, 'the favorite Paramount hangout'; a Paramount lawyer served legal papers on Redford during the lunch. That ended that.

Meanwhile John Cassavetes informally petitioned Castle for the part. Many felt that Cassavetes wasn't right for the 'all-American husband'; he looked too dishonest and shifty from the start. Levin shared these doubts: 'I had some questions about John Cassavetes, only because he's so devilish that you suspect him. He was fine, but I think he gave it away a little, just by that twinkle in his eyes.'[39] In the end, it was Polanski who opted for Cassavetes:

With Redford and Beatty ruled out, we lowered our sights. John Cassavetes, whom I'd met in London and regarded as a 'cerebral' actor, struck me as an acceptable compromise. Evans expressed doubts when I recommended him for the part, saying he was too much of a 'heavy' and that he was also known to be trouble on the set. I disregarded this and felt he'd make a workmanlike job of it.[40]

Perhaps they were right to wonder about his aptness for the role. Yet Polanski's decision to go with him undoubtedly opened up new possibilities for the movie, as Cassavetes's contradictorily productive cinematic and acting style in other ways galvanized Polanski's film.

Born in 1929, Cassavetes was the son of a Greek immigrant, a New Yorker who had spent his early childhood in Greece. An experimenter in acting and film-making, he was a natural independent. He was wolfish, physical, a palpable son-of-a-bitch. The careful, designed process of film-making frustrated him; he wanted more freedom in his performances, something 'zany, comical and madcap'.[41] With his collaborator Burt Lane, he developed an acting method based on the idea that we all employ masks, a 'personality mask'. This was an idea that could usefully feed into an understanding of Guy Woodhouse – a man who is all mask and has no face at all.

John Cassavetes in the studio with Shafi Hadi, recording the music for *Shadows* (1959).

Cassavetes came into the project as a big name. In 1959, he had directed his first film, *Shadows*, a substantial critical success. In 1967, he was nominated for an Oscar for Best Supporting Actor for *The Dirty Dozen*. He had not wanted to be in the film, thinking it 'the wrong movie in the wrong country at the wrong time', but really liked working with its director, Robert Aldrich. More usually, he was busy selling his soul for roles he didn't like or enjoy, to finance the making of his own films.

He got on well with Aldrich, but he was far from getting on well with everyone. He relished his own spikiness, using aggression to be 'real'; Don Siegel once suggested that 'Cassavetes seemed to treat every encounter as a test of his manhood.'[42] He was famous for transforming everyday scenes into assaults, intimidating Lillian Ross, throwing Pauline Kael's shoes out of a mid-town taxi on the way to a reception, even bullying his wife, Gena Rowlands. He would risk judgement and embarrassment, rather than tone himself down for a social self. His aggression, his distance and emotional inaccessibility would all pour directly into Guy.

The others in the coven

One of *Rosemary's Baby*'s strengths lies in its supporting cast, one that brought to this modish movie key figures from Hollywood's golden age. 'Old' Hollywood here merges with the new, incorporating faces recognizable from the American past. Other than Guy and Rosemary, the first character we see is Mr Nicklas, played by Elisha Cook, recalled from *The Maltese Falcon* (1941), *The Big Sleep* (1946) and *Shane* (1953), a remembered man, embedded in popular culture history.

To cast the movie, Polanski sketched his idea of what the characters should look like. These drawings were worked up by a Paramount artist, 'and Hoyt Bowers, who headed the casting department still maintained by Paramount in those spacious days, set about matching them. This was how we came to hire such old-timers

Patsy Kelly as Laura-Louise.

as Ralph Bellamy, Sydney Blackmer, Elisha Cook and Patsy Kelly, none of whom I'd seen on the screen for years.'[43]

Patsy Kelly was reportedly Polanski's idea; one key to grasping the film is the fact that, coming out of vaudeville, she was primarily known for comedy, the 1930s' 'Queen of the Wisecracks'. Famous for *The Awful Truth* (1937) and *His Girl Friday* (1940), Ralph Bellamy as Dr Sapirstein brought another kind of comedic distinction to the movie. Bellamy was also chosen in part for his resemblance to Castle. He even went to Castle's tailor, Frank Hoffer, to copy the producer's style of clothes.[44] The quality of these people undoubtedly enriched the film. Polanski remarked of these old Hollywood actors – 'I am using them for the simple reason that they are good.'[45]

Designs for living

When it came to the crew for the film, Polanski was already clear on one thing: he wanted Richard Sylbert as his production designer. He even lent Sylbert the galleys of the novel before he had started to adapt it. Polanski admired his work as art director on Elia Kazan's *Baby Doll* (1956); the two had already met in London.[46] Polanski was thrilled to work with him, 'because the real star of the picture

would be the New York apartment where Rosemary and Guy go to live'.[47] Born in 1928, Sylbert was, like Evans and Castle, a native of Brooklyn. In 1967, he was still finishing his work on Mike Nichols's *The Graduate* in California, while already scouting locations for *Rosemary's Baby* in New York. As we shall see, for the main location he chose the Dakota building on the corner of Central Park West and 72nd Street.[48] On Sylbert's recommendation, Anthea Sylbert, his sister-in-law designed the costumes.

Polanski and Sylbert spent thirty days going through the script at Polanski's Californian beach-house.[49] In Paramount Studios, Sylbert went about fabricating the Woodhouse and Castevet apartments. The design miraculously imparts a sense of solidity to the space; in fact the walls were only attached by catches and could come apart to make room for the cameras. To mimic the proportions of the Dakota, the walls on set were eighteen to twenty feet high. (Set walls are usually eight to ten feet high.) The windows overlooked a background plate of Central Park.[50] Dick Sylbert and William ('Bill') Fraker, the cinematographer, exploited lighting to suggest changing times of day. The Woodhouse home becomes a model of stylish interior design, a counter to the Castevets's nouveau riche and 'gaudy' apartment.[51] Foregoing the move towards shooting in real locations, for much of the film Polanski's characters live in a studio-bound world, a place of pure artifice. Marvellously designed by Joel Schiller, for Rosemary's dream scenic designer Clem Hall did the actual building of the Sistine Frescoes, conjuring the apartment into a Vatican chapel. They worked with plastic paint on canvas with plaster texture; reproducing one quarter of the original paintings, it took six weeks and cost $200 000 to build.[52] The aim throughout, with costumes and the set, was to put people at their ease by using the 'garish' to inject a dash of the real into this Manhattan fairy tale.

Shoot the Devil

Shooting for *Rosemary's Baby* began in New York on 21 August 1967.[53] They followed a 56-day schedule, with the interiors to be done in Los Angeles and the exteriors in Manhattan. Before shooting began the cast rehearsed the film like a play. Then the crew moved to New York for the outdoor scenes. William A. Fraker, the cinematographer, was one of the Hollywood greats; he would go on to be nominated for five Oscars for cinematography and one for visual effects. Fraker shot the film with a '50-speed color negative film, one camera and 18 and 25 mm lenses (the latter mainly for handheld, close-up shots of the actors)'.[54] David Walsh was camera-operator on the film. At Dick Sylbert's suggestions, rather than be lumbered with one of Castle's editors, the movie would be edited by the amazingly talented Sam O'Steen and his assistant, Bob Wyman.

On the first day of shooting at the Dakota, they filmed Guy and Rosemary arriving at 'the Bramford' and the discovery of Terry's body on the sidewalk. Elia Kazan, the great director of *On The Waterfront* (1954), came out to watch; he lived across the street.[55]

Farrow was absolutely dedicated to the part. As the script demanded, she ate raw liver, even though she was then a committed vegetarian. In New York, to expose Rosemary's distraction, very early on in the shooting Polanski had Farrow step out for real with him into the path of the oncoming traffic on Park Avenue: '"Nobody will hit a pregnant woman," he laughed, referring to my padded stomach. He had to operate the hand-held camera himself, since nobody else

Mia Farrow with Roman Polanski about to make their dash across 5th Avenue.

would.' They did the shot three times.[56] 'There are 127 varieties of nuts,' he told a journalist, 'Mia's 116 of them.'[57]

In the rape scene, Cassavetes was naked, but among the coven Mia Farrow, Patsy Kelly and Ruth Gordon were not nude, the latter two being clad in body-suits. For the majority of this scene, a stand-in, Linda Brewerton, was used to substitute for Farrow.[58] Polanski said soon afterwards, about the scene where she is tied down: 'I can't even remember if the legs are Mia Farrow's or those of the stand-in we used at times to give the star a rest.'[59] When the scene was finished, Clay Tanner, the actor playing the Devil, climbed off Farrow and courteously remarked, '"Miss Farrow, I just want to say, it's a real pleasure to have worked with you".'[60]

With his customary flair, Castle transformed Farrow's ultra-fashionable Vidal Sassoon haircut into a publicity event. Castle stood in as the Sapirstein lookalike lurking outside the phone booth while Rosemary calls Dr Hill. (This was the first dialogue scene shot for the movie.) There are possibilities that this doubling was merely fortuitous, or that Castle relished the Hitchcock shtick of appearing in his own films. However, as we shall see, this moment ties into a tendency in the movie to make in-jokes about its own status as a film.

Footage and photographs of the shooting show how well Farrow and Polanski got on, playing ping-pong on set, making up 'Mia's Chart', a jokey way of monitoring the actor's technical accomplishment with grades. Farrow was winsomely (or irritatingly) childlike, dancing, painting, playing. Documentary footage also reveals how concentratedly attentive the director was to the process of filming. Yet for three reasons the shoot was not altogether a smooth one.

Afterwards, Polanski welcomed Castle's lack of interference, something he put down to the older man not being a frustrated film-maker.[61] In fact, the producer had been hot for Polanski to be fired from the film. The youthful director was all too meticulous. There were reputedly fifty-two takes of the laundry-room scene; for Polanski to do forty takes of a scene became usual. Polanski

Elia Kazan looks on as Polanski directs on the first night's shooting of *Rosemary's Baby*; Farrow, Polanski, Castle on-set with Joan Crawford.

was filming in long, complicated shots, in which everything had to come together perfectly. After one week's shooting, they were one week behind schedule; bad weather slowed the shoot in New York down too.[62] The schedule stretched to fourteen weeks; they spent two weeks in New York. Watching him that first night, Kazan had thought him slow. Polanski was a perfectionist, and Castle and Bluhdorn were growing desperate. To Bluhdorn's indignant scorn, Polanski rejected a red cab sent to drive Rosemary to Hutch's funeral, and held up filming while someone fetched a proper New York yellow cab; authenticity in the film's details was vital. Evans resolved the dispute with Castle and the executives by pointing out the quality of the material that Polanski was filming. Yet for a while, as would often happen with Polanski, it was touch and go if he'd finish the film at all. They went over their $2.3 million budget; but then again the film would eventually make a little under $34 million.[63] Polanski remembers meeting Otto Preminger on the set; Preminger reassured him that no-one was ever fired for going over-budget.[64] In the end, of course, the movie itself, and its enormous profits, vindicated Polanski.

Moreover, the movie threw Sinatra and Farrow's marriage into crisis. Sinatra resented Farrow's stardom, and wanted her to finish it on time and join him, as a dutiful wife should, on the set of *The Detective* at Fox studios in mid-October. Instead the shooting dragged and Sinatra grew increasingly frustrated. In the end, Farrow had to finish by 14 November, with her shooting on *The Detective* set to begin three days later. Sinatra threatened to pull Farrow out of Polanski's movie, and thereby effectively shut it down. Farrow was left with a stark choice: if she didn't leave *Rosemary's Baby*, her marriage was over; if she did leave, her career was over. Sinatra's lawyer, Mickey Rudin, came to the Paramount set to deliver the divorce papers. Afterwards Mia retreated to her mobile dressing room, sobbing her heart out.[65] As Evans tells it, he persuaded Farrow to stay with the movie by suggesting an Oscar was on the cards.[66] While reacting to the stress of these events, Farrow did the movie's final scene where she confronts the hostile, elderly witches and sees her own terrible child, the anguish on camera a reflection of her genuine distress. Farrow commented later, 'I applied myself to the remainder of the movie with a fervor usually reserved for prayer.'[67]

The third problem was Cassavetes. During the rehearsals, the actor had been friendly enough, but he became increasingly difficult as filming began. Polanski began to question the actor's ability to go beyond himself and play another person. Cassavetes objected to the scene where Guy and Rosemary made love, 'protesting that he wasn't "in the skin flick business." Mia was equally reluctant to do this scene, but for a different and more understandable reason: she felt apprehensive about Sinatra's reactions.'[68]

During filming, the many takes undoubtedly frustrated Cassavetes, who disliked repetition, and felt that the actors were losing the freshness and the space to play out the emotion. Each day, the actor came to work with fresh ideas about his role; each day, Polanski dismissed them.[69] Perhaps Cassavetes bore a grudge about Polanski's power and celebrity, and disliked the way in which his own role in the film faded as it went on. The anger racked up. The two men argued about the movie and they argued about love.[70] As he would often do, Cassavetes was likely using contention and strife to deepen his performance. Moreover, in a film about manipulation and suppression, Cassavetes was rather aptly voicing a protest about being directed at all. Fraker reports that:

One day we were working and all of a sudden we heard this screaming and hollering, and John came out from behind the set and started walking away to the stage door. He was screaming, 'There are no stars in this goddamn picture. You're the star.' And Roman stuck his head out from behind the set and said, 'You better believe it!'

Eventually, Cassavetes lost his grip completely, and there was screaming, fury, and the two men fought it out, until cast and crew separated them.[71]

Afterwards Cassavetes would prove intriguingly equivocal about the movie and Polanski. He could at times suggest that the film was not art, merely a 'dictated design', but, despite their conflict on set, he consistently praised Polanski and even declared that he would like to work with him again.[72] On the other hand, Polanski became increasingly dismissive of Cassavetes; soon after the film was finished, he remarked in an interview that Cassavetes 'was not a filmmaker – he's made some films'; worse, he was a twisted, overwrought actor (*très tordu*), but that he'd been punished or purged (*châtié*) by the editing.[73]

In December 1967, the cast and crew returned to New York to film the Christmas scene out on Fifth Avenue. It was 6 December, and it was the last scene they shot.

2 The Turn

Plots

Both Levin's novel and Polanski's film unravel substantially the same plot.[1] Rosemary (Mia Farrow) and her husband, a struggling young actor, Guy Woodhouse (John Cassavetes), are shown an apartment to rent in Bramford Apartments. The previous owner, Mrs Gardenia, a retired lawyer, died and left it vacant. The Woodhouses decide to take the apartment, renovate the place, and move in. We hear from Rosemary's old friend, Hutch (Maurice Evans), a writer of adventure stories for boys, that the building, an old block of flats in New York City, had a bad reputation for witchcraft and cannibalism at the turn of the century, when Adrian Marcato attempted to conjure up the Devil in the building; when people heard what he had done, he was torn to pieces by a mob in the lobby.

The Woodhouses' immediate neighbours are an elderly couple, the Castevets, Roman (Sidney Blackmer) and Minnie (Ruth Gordon). Rosemary meets Terry (Angela Dorian), a girl of her own age whom the Castevets have befriended. After an evening out, Rosemary and Guy return to find Terry's dead body on the sidewalk, surrounded by police and onlookers after a suicide or tragic fall. Rosemary offers her condolences to Minnie and Roman. Minnie drops around to Rosemary's apartment to invite the young pair to dinner. Guy and the elderly couple become very friendly. Guy hears that the actor, Donald Baumgart, who landed a part Guy had wanted has mysteriously gone blind; consequently Guy is offered the role. Guy rehearses, and becomes pensive and remote, spending more and more time with the Castevets. He apologizes, and suggests that they try immediately, as Rosemary has long wanted, for a baby.

On the night they plan to conceive their child, Rosemary passes out; she dreams she is raped by Satan at a black mass. Next morning, she wakes to find scratches on her body, and Guy apologizes, declaring he had sex with her while she was unconscious. Rosemary's pregnancy is a very hard one, controlled by her neighbours and their friend, Dr Sapirstein (Ralph Bellamy). The Castevets confine and coddle Rosemary; on his way to warn Rosemary about something, Hutch falls into a coma.

Months pass. The due date is only a few weeks away. Rosemary hears that Hutch has died. She receives a cryptic message from him, which she decodes as a warning that her neighbours are witches and Roman Castevet is in fact Steven Marcato, the son of the Bramford's black magician, and that they are perhaps intending harm to her baby. Rosemary realizes that Guy and Dr Sapirstein are also part of the coven. She attempts to escape, but is captured by 'the witches' and drugged; when she wakes it is to find that her baby boy has been born and is well. Suddenly, the child is said to be dead, but Rosemary finds him in a black-draped cradle with an inverted crucifix on it and the coven celebrating around him. She's told that the child is Satan's son. Compelled by maternal instinct, Rosemary finds herself rocking the baby.

Music from another room

The film begins with the Paramount logo and some harsh, fractured piano notes, and then ushers in a lullaby. The music was written by the extraordinarily talented Polish jazz-musician and composer, the reserved and gentle Krzysztof Komeda (1931–1969). Born Krzysztof Trzci, he studied for six years at the Polish Medical Academy (becoming an 'ear, nose, throat, and neck' specialist). He adopted Komeda as his stage-name in 1956 when he became a jazz musician. One year later he met Polanski for the first time. As well as his consistently excellent work scoring most of Polanski's early films, he also provided the music for Henning Carlsen's *Hunger* (1966) and Jerzy Skolimowski's *Barrier* (1966) and *The Departure* (1967), among others.

The reverberating piano that opens *Rosemary's Baby* strikes the note of a doubled world, a place of echoes.[2] For much of the film,

Komeda's music plays out a dark version of a pop Henry Mancini score. It is part cool jazz, part spectral unease, with music that descends from romance to dread. Later the music turns to dissonance, and an almost unbearable tension, as Rosemary races to the apparent safety of her apartment. Most striking of all is the wordless lullaby that begins and ends the film, and that is reinvented and remoulded so many times in between. Sung by Farrow, that lullaby returns us both to the maternal comforts and to the uncanny fears belonging to the realm of childhood, its lilting cosiness jolted by discords.[3]

A New York state of mind

So often New York lives in movies as the locale of reinvention, a place premised on freedom. Yet in *Rosemary's Baby*, it is a constricted city and the site of hidden persecutions. Instilled with indeterminate menace, the film's opening shots are one of the few moments when the urban context for Rosemary's isolated oppression appears.[4] We see the New York that we hardly glimpse again as the metropolis spreads out before us. This will also be the last shot we see, the camera returning at the close to a vantage point above the city, where all stories seem equal, and no one is clearly seen. When it came to finding a double for the Bramford Apartment block, Brooklynite

Sylbert already knew they must choose the Dakota. After all, alongside the Osborne (apparently once Levin's home in New York), Levin namechecks the Dakota in his novel as a better alternative to the Bramford.[5]

Rosemary's Baby is a city film, one of the greatest, a story intimately tied to the cultural image of New York. It grants us a perverse version of Holly Golightly's city (one cut scene was to be set at the stationery counter in Tiffany's), a city of promise for a young woman – though here that promise turns very sour. Tightness and enclosure fascinate Polanski, whose films from *Knife in the Water* to *Carnage* replay the dilemmas of people shut in together. Like many great city films of the sixties (*The Servant* [1963], *Performance* [1970], *The Odd Couple*, *The Apartment* [1960]), urban experience plays out largely within the confines of a single locale. The apartment proves to be a microcosm of the city. Outside almost vanishes. When cutting down the movie, Sam O'Steen edited out most exterior moments, all those instances where Rosemary stepped beyond, met friends, seemed free. While most of the 'New Hollywood' movies opted for the open road or lit out for the frontier, Polanski moved inwards, setting up an agoraphobic America.[6]

Rosemary's Baby tells the story of two apartments that were once in fact the same apartment but are now divided and doubled – 'Originally the smallest apartment was a nine – they've been broken into fours, fives, and sixes.'[7] The Castevets's apartment, Victorian, gloomy, ornate, haunts Rosemary's bright, clean, modernized home. History broods in Gothic and imbues the architecture of New York. One world spies on another; when Rosemary and Guy first come to the apartment, a nosy workman is drilling a peephole in another apartment's front-door. Beyond this dark dyad of the Castevets and the Woodhouses, there are the other realms of the film, all sites of transit or dead-end places of threat – the basement, the elevator, the exposed and unsafe streets.

The film's soundscape summons up this sense of a porous place. Like many apartments, we are privy to voices and noises from other

rooms. Sounds permeate the house. Someone practises Beethoven's
'Für Elise', a childhood memory for Polanski.[8] Via the telephone,
people invade the house from outside; children play beyond, jets
pass overhead, there's traffic sounds, and above all through the walls
there's Minnie's voice, her constant admonishment of her muted
husband, the neighbours' marriage present in their house too.

A modern couple

Rosemary's Baby plays out as a gradually darkening soap opera
(Farrow was, after all, fresh from *Peyton Place*); it begins like
Barefoot in the Park and ends like *Confessions of a Justified Sinner*.
The link to *Barefoot in the Park* is not a flip one: that film's star,
Robert Redford, after all, was first choice to play Guy, and Farrow
reportedly believed that Jane Fonda, its female lead, had been first
choice for Rosemary.[9] (*Barefoot in the Park* had been Paramount
Pictures' big hit of the spring and summer of 1967.) Yet in *Barefoot*,

Robert Redford and Jane Fonda, modern lovers, in *Barefoot in the Park*.

Rosemary and Guy, a fashionable couple.

Jane Fonda plays a stroppy homemaker, someone making a bourgeois space while insisting that it also be bohemian. Rosemary is far more conventional: she spends her time apologizing for or rounding off her appalling husband, and has no possibility of a career for herself. She has been trapped in the feminine mystique, but (apparently) contentedly so, as though happiness consists of seeming to live in a colour Sunday supplement world.

At the start, Rosemary and Guy stroll through the courtyard of the Bramford, hand in hand, well-heeled and chic, a Technicolor couple in Polanski's first Technicolor film. They're migrants to the city, Rosemary from Omaha and Guy from Baltimore, ready to partake in its sophisticated glamour. These modern lovers are happy consumers. Rosemary herself will, in time, become a commodity, a bargaining chip in someone else's bargain. If Guy sells his 'talent' to advertisers, Rosemary isn't even allowed to sell herself. Instead she is sold; Guy plays a Faust who offers up another person's soul.

Rosemary's first step is to decorate the apartment, to make her own set. The quaint old-fashioned space of Mrs Gardenia's turn-of-the-century home becomes *en vogue*. However, meeting Hutch, they quickly learn that the history of certain places may not be simply dispelled by a lick of paint and a trip to Barneys. They are in the 'Black Bramford', a place with a particularly Gothic history. Besides Adrian Marcato, it takes in the Trench sisters (cannibalistic former tenants), Keith Kennedy with his 'parties', and the mysterious Pearl Ames. These 'historical' figures belong to fiction but impart a suggestion of 'real' crimes; the viewer cannot help but wonder how real they might be. The idea arises that a place might in itself be 'malign', malevolence built into the fabric of the walls.

Aren't you Victoria Vetri?

However, if New York history embodies itself in 'the Bram', it does so as theatre and performance. The Bram's not just a historical space, it is a stage-set. The real estate agent boasts that they have a lot of actors residing there. Like the Bramford, the Dakota was a place for stars: Lauren Bacall lived there with Jason Robards; Boris Karloff grew orchids on the top floor.

When Rosemary goes down to the basement to do her laundry, and initiates a conversation with her neighbour, by asking, 'Aren't you Victoria Vetri', the young woman, Terry Gionoffrio, replies that she gets mistaken for that actress a lot. Of course, though going under her Playboy bunny name, Angela Dorian (she was Playmate of the Month that September, even as these scenes were being shot),

Angela Dorian a.k.a. Victoria Vetri as Terry Gionoffrio.

the actor herself really is Victoria Vetri, and the character is being taken for the person truly playing her. This cinematic referencing was there already in Levin's novel, where the young woman resembles Anna Maria Alberghetti, star of *Ten Thousand Bedrooms* (1957) and *Cinderfella* (1960). (In Polanski's script, when Rosemary kisses the Pope's ring during the dream of the rape, 'Inside it, ANNA MARIA ALBERGHETTI sits waiting.') For Levin, both the coven's would-be surrogate mothers take after movie-stars, with Rosemary having a look, as mentioned above, of Piper Laurie.

This quip about Victoria Vetri alludes to the fact that it is a film and the players merely players. In the novel, and referenced in the movie, Rosemary pays a visit to a theatre in Greenwich Village, catching Tom Jones's *The Fantasticks*, a musical (that ran off-Broadway for forty-two years) about the manipulation of children by their parents to enforce their will regarding marriage. Later Mia Farrow talks on the phone to Donald Baumgart, played, although she did not know it, by her uncredited film-star friend, Tony Curtis; stand-ins impersonate the Pope and the Catholic Kennedys. (In the dream on the yacht, JFK's voice is pure Vaughan Meader.) The director shares a first name with the head of the coven, and a nickname ('Ro') with the young woman they oppress. (In an interview in 1969, Polanski suggests that Levin had used 'Roman' because he was alluding to *Repulsion*, and therefore already thinking of Polanski; he goes on to add that Levin 'categorically denied it'.[10]) Complexities ramify and identities amalgamate: Castevet echoes Cassavetes; Mia shortens 'Maria', the Virgin Mother that Rosemary may blasphemously reincarnate.

The threatening figure looming outside the phone booth is Castle, the movie's horror-film producer. And after all, in the plot Roman Castevet acts as a producer, effectively replicating William Castle's role. The Castevets deride Catholicism as mere 'show business'; moreover, in some of its American manifestations, the Satanism of the period was self-consciously theatrical. The founder of the Church of Satan, Anton LaVey remarked, 'Witchcraft has a lot of

show business in it.'[11] In Roman Castevet's words, Adrian Marcato's
Satanic religion masquerades as the work of a 'theatrical producer'.
For all the film's realism, the Gothic draws on a style that is in essence
something unreal, something palpably artificial.

This self-consciousness is a sixties trope, part of an era of
metafiction, of John Fowles and B.S. Johnson. The world of the actors
and those of the characters lean into each other. After all, it suggests,
what's religion and politics but show business and advertising dream?
The strongest way that this theatrical theme enters into the film is
through Guy, his profession and his shifty, shifting persona. There's
a bumptious, cocky, self-absorbed, sarcastic restlessness in him; he is
constantly over-emphatic, constantly not really there, troubled by the
direction of his life, and yet ready to impose on others.

The first line in Polanski's script has the real estate agent
Mr Nicklas saying 'Oh, an actor', clearly a response to something
already said.[12] From the start, Guy is someone playacting through
life. In the movie itself, the first words we hear Guy saying are a
lie – Mr Nicklas asks, 'Are you a doctor?' 'Yes,' Guy instantly replies.
'He's an actor,' Rosemary says, putting an end to Guy's little play.
Guy then lies directly again, this time about the plays he's been in.
He's a mimic man, impersonating Mr Nicklas, impersonating Minnie.

With Mr Nicklas, he breaks into an impression of Richard Burton.[13] We feel all this mimicry as a pledge of insecurity and a form of contempt, a way of arrogantly not being yourself and of aggressively suggesting others cannot be anything else.

People here are performers, or those who get others to perform for them. For Steven Marcato, 'Roman Castevet' is a part he plays. The film suggests that an actor, such as Guy, may be no more than a licensed liar. Guy has performed in *Nobody Loves an Albatross*, a real play, by Ronald Alexander, that ran on Broadway from December 1963 to June 1964. Like *Rosemary's Baby*, the play examines the suspect nature of acting and fame, delving into the US television industry and the desperate crawl towards success. (This is a film whose characters are shown, time and again, watching television.) He's also been in John Osborne's *Luther*, which ran at the St James's Theatre, New York, from September 1963, with Albert Finney in the leading role. In other words, Guy was very busy three years ago but has not done much since, except to sell his talent for advertising. As a consequence, Guy relishes 'networking' and making contacts; Levin tells us he tolerates Rosemary's friendship with Hutch, because Hutch knows Terence Rattigan: 'Connections often proved crucial in the theatre.'[14]

This theatrical theme entwines itself with the movie's investigation of the relationship between men and women. It scrutinizes the directorial relationship, the intertwining of actor and director, as a kind of mirror for marriage. After all, Polanski was an actor and director soon to marry a woman he had directed and Cassavetes was an actor and director married to Gena Rowlands, whom he was busy directing in *Faces* (1968). Marriage reproduces the relationship between director and actor, but also between parent and child; Mia Farrow's father was the film director, John Farrow, married to Maureen O'Sullivan, also an actress he had directed. It makes sense for a relation to seem like theatre, where couples, after all, have 'scenes' ('if it's going to turn into a big scene'). In scene after scene in Levin's novel, Rosemary wonders if she can trust what she sees of Guy: 'He was an actor; could anyone know when an actor was true and not acting?' It's a dilemma that undercuts Cassavetes's doctrine of 'authenticity' at the root. On hearing about Donald Baumgart's blindness, Guy dwindles into a synthetic person: 'He sat motionless, his hand staying on the phone. He was pale and dummylike, a Pop Art wax statue with real clothes and props, a real phone, real can of paint remover.'[15] On film the props are real, and the person is merely an image. Andy Warhol's Factory was only twenty-five cross-streets away.

Guy's Faustian compact follows a purely professional anxiety. At a time when jobs were for life, the professions respected and unions strong, the actor was already living in the future of precariousness we all now inhabit. The actor moves between unemployment and temporary jobs, living on his or her wits. They live by pleasing, and, in the end, if they fail to please, it's all over. Guy strives merely to keep things rolling; he corrupts himself to gain a security that in fact will only last as long as the next job.

What truly makes Guy consent to Roman and Minnie's proposition? It might seem that Guy does not so much wish to be a famous actor, as he longs for the destruction of his rival and, above all, for the degradation of his wife. The bargain is not a means to an end, it is the end in itself. The pact he makes is one that would appear to have occurred between men, in a parody of business meetings, secured with the sharing of manly cigars; it is Roman who coaxes him, while Minnie washes up. The deal expresses all Guy's barely suppressed enmity towards Rosemary. Guy yearns for temptation per se, for its self-importance; he wishes to play Faust. Rosemary lives as his soul and his Gretchen, her given-over body the present sign of the personhood from which he would free himself. Disposing her as a property signals his mastery; she is subsumed into him, one flesh, her will his own, her womb his commodity.

The odd couple

Terry Gionoffrio lies crushed and bleeding on the sidewalk, and from out of the New York summer night, an old couple approaches from the street. Polanski's script puts their entry into the film this way: they are brassy, 'dazzling' in their vulgarity, aged but 'with expressions of young alertness', withered, but Roman's mouth is 'rosy-pink, as if lipsticked'.[16] From their entrance into the film, the action will be instigated by these lurid, elderly anti-heroes.

Polanski had suggested Alfred Lunt and Joan Fontaine for Roman and Minnie. However, while having lunch Castle had bumped into Sidney Blackmer, with a toupee (which, to see if he'd be physically right for the role, Castle made him wear back to front).[17] Blackmer was another member of the old Hollywood guard; he was especially famous for playing Theodore Roosevelt (he did so a dozen times), and brought something of that charisma and poise to the commanding Roman Castevet.

Polanski knew Ruth Gordon from more recent films, though with some justice he hated *Inside Daisy Clover* (1965), her latest movie (for which she had received an Oscar nomination).[18] Some are immune to Gordon's acerbic charm; one critic suggested that Gordon 'plays all parts exactly the same, without fear or favour, in a style that doesn't remotely suit any of them'.[19] Moreover, she differed significantly from Levin's description of Minnie, the writer seeing her as 'a big woman'.[20] However, Levin was persuaded, as Polanski was, that, short as she was, 'Ruth proved extraordinarily effective as a small, birdlike, quintessential New Yorker.'[21] She's a jauntily sly presence in the film. Farrow and Ruth Gordon were well acquainted. When Farrow was taken up by Vivien Leigh, while playing in *The Importance of Being Earnest*, Ruth Gordon was with Leigh. Moreover, Gordon and her husband Garson Kanin were also friends of Sinatra's; the pair even attended Farrow and Sinatra's wedding party.[22]

Gordon had married Kanin in 1942; he was her second husband. They were a great Hollywood couple, writing together Katharine Hepburn and Spencer Tracy's *Adam's Rib* (1949) and *Pat and Mike* (1953) and (also for George Cukor) *A Double Life* (1948). Kanin also was one of the collaborators on Cukor's *Woman of the*

Ruth Gordon as Minnie in costume for Hal Ashby's *Harold and Maude* (1971).

Year (1942), making the two of them experts in the problems and possibilities of a modern, equal marriage.

On screen, Gordon comes across as quaint or eccentric; the rumours go that she was in fact 'very difficult and rather horrible. If you feel tempted to regard her as a sweet old lady, or a sprightly "character", then beware the sudden swoop of witch or mystic.'[23] It's the combination of the two possibilities that make Minnie so powerful a presence.

To speak of woe that is in marriage

In *Rosemary's Baby*, relatedness marks itself out as indistinguishable from coercion. The Castevets create another version of what marriage might be, the only other example that the movie presents. They are a shadow couple, a double for the Woodhouses' dire marriage. The film investigates the condition of modern marriage, analysing a crisis in relations between the sexes, where what is at stake is the conflict between independence and control.

When Guy comes home from work, disappointed and wearied, and finds that Rosemary has agreed to have dinner with the neighbours, a revelatory exchange takes place. He sulkily asks if they really must go; Rosemary perkily says, no, of course they don't, implicitly getting across through the faux cheerfulness that she's put out; Guy relents and says then they'll go; Rosemary says, no, they don't have to go; and Guy insists that they must. And the film cuts to their arriving for dinner. It's a note-perfect instance of something we find often in their relation to each other. For their marriage founds itself on a softly reticent, mutual, passive-aggressive manipulation. She gets Guy to go to dinner; later he'll do his best to get her, through moral pressure, to eat up her chocolate mousse, change her obstetrician, put up with months of pain and so on. Her few decisions that thwart him – her close-cropped Vidal Sassoon haircut, a party– are small adolescent rebellions, assertions of will in a place where the will is compromised. There are other such relations. Above all, Minnie manipulates her too, enforcing her way through guilt and social obligation. Rosemary can be charmingly, irritatingly, childlike, not least in being someone controlled, someone made guilty.

The film pits men against young women, with the older women acting as enablers of a sexual status quo that tyrannizes over and belittles them. Family life itself can seem a conspiracy here, an entrapment in the generations. Guy consistently fails to understand Rosemary, perpetually shows himself unable to feel compassion for her. Most viewers to the film feel hostile towards Guy; when she spits in his face at the end, I have heard audiences voice their long-delayed satisfaction. His name, Guy, signals his banality, and perhaps his typicality as a man; he's just some guy, an everyman.

Guy and Rosemary act like father and daughter, in a relationship that becomes increasingly, after the conception, sexless. From the start sex appears perfunctory. When they make love in the newly acquired apartment, the intimacy seems peculiarly banal; as a French critic puts it: 'Elle dit: "Let's make love" – son mari fait, "Hum, hum", ils se déshabbilent et voilà'.[24] In their marriage, sex is either blank or brutal or absent. That first sex scene in any case stops short, as Guy interrupts the moment with a joke about the Trench sisters munching, one kind of consumption overlaying another. One of the scenes present in the script but cut from the film has Rosemary

ROSEMARY'S BABY | 49

and Guy telling each other, 'I love you.'[25] Lost from the movie, the word 'love' never in fact passes between them.

The Woodhouse marriage may be a counterpart to Farrow's actual marriage and its 29-year age-gap. Character and actor merge, just as, in the public's mind, Mia had entwined with Allison, the part she played in *Peyton Place*. Mia's Allison was described in *The New York Times* as 'some girl Oedipus … on the brink of discovery'.[26] Due to *Peyton Place*, Farrow more normally figured in the public mind as a daughter; here, in *Rosemary's Baby* she's the daughter as mother-to-be. Her parents are absent, perhaps pointedly uninterested in a Catholic daughter who's married an agnostic Protestant. Instead there is Hutch, English and fifty-four years old; in the novel, Levin specifically says he's 'the full-time father-substitute'.[27] Then Minnie and Roman supplant that role. Hutch tells Roman, 'You and your wife seem to be taking better care of Rosemary than her own parents would.' And Rosemary tells him, 'Guy's gotten very close to them … I think they've become sort of parent-figures for him.' As Joan Didion had described the hippy kids doing in *Slouching Towards Bethlehem*, Rosemary and Guy are busy forming extended families in their absence.[28]

Guy too can seem more of a father than a husband. There's sixteen years between them, not so much perhaps, but enough, given Rosemary's youth, to place them in different realms. There are other such relationships here, mirroring the Woodhouses' set-up: at the funeral, we find that Hutch's daughter, Doris Hutchins, is married to a man rather older than her own father; in the novel, we learn that Roman is some twelve years older than Minnie. (It may be indirectly pertinent that Sylbert and O'Steen had both worked on *The Graduate* (1967), and that Ruth Gordon's next film, *Harold and Maude*, pushes the age-gap relation as far as it will go, though benignly, and with the woman as the older partner.) There are Oedipal tensions here. As Guy prepares Rosemary for the rape, he soothes her with a 'Ro, baby,' a 'You'll be alright, baby.' Moreover, when Rosemary feigns to have eaten up her dessert, a child's ruse, she asks Guy, 'Do I get a gold star, daddy?' And when she breaks the news of her pregnancy to Guy, she calls him 'father', and he responds, 'mother'.

As we'll later see, in a film released in 1968, the presence of age and youth as themes in the film carried vital political resonances too.

The Pope in Yankee Stadium

While he was writing the novel, Levin discovered that the night of Rosemary's conception coincided with the Pope's officiating Mass at Yankee Stadium. It was a serendipitous link that gathered up the story's entwinement with Catholic ritual and Christian myth.[29] *Rosemary's Baby* is both a film that mocks Catholicism and a Catholic film. This is despite the fact that both Levin and Polanski were agnostics, and uncomfortable with the movie's endorsement of a supernatural realm. Polanski later described himself as 'very uneasy about making a serious film about the devil. I thought it was silly somehow, that's why I left it ambiguous.'[30] While some feel profound shock or discomfort about the Satanic presence in the film, Polanski himself was apparently indifferent to it.

However, the movie may bear some faint traces of its director's long-forgotten Catholic phase. His mother's family were Catholic converts and Polanski in early youth thought of himself as a Catholic ('When I prayed, I still prayed as a Catholic') – until it became apparent that as far as his fellow Poles were concerned he was not allowed to be one.[31] Likewise, as part of the film's riffing on the real lives of its actors, especially its main female star, Farrow had herself had a strict Catholic upbringing. At the time, Farrow was known as a devotee of the new spiritual paths; soon after the movie's release, she flew with her sister Prudence Farrow to Rishikesh in India to learn from the Maharishi Mahesh Yogi. However, Farrow's education imbued her late-1960s spirituality: 'It makes a stamp on you, the Catholic upbringing. It's tattooed on your soul,' she remarked.[32]

On its release, critics noted a central paradox in the film, as its unsettling depictions of Satanic ritual and its assertion of the power of evil nonetheless carry some nostalgic force, summoning

up a world in which religious certainties still pertain.[33] In *The New York Times*, Renata Adler named it, 'a highly serious lapsed-Catholic fable'. As Polanski remarked, in accepting that the Devil exists, you necessarily accept God exists.[34] In a world without belief, the witches are the last believers, and all Rosemary can do to maintain her faith is to believe in them. The movie shares in the essential equivocation of blasphemy, that inverting or perverting the sacred nonetheless bears witness to the sacred it would smear. Parody operates as a derivative mode; it follows after. Even the reported death of God alluded to in the film must follow His life. 'God is dead' means something quite other than 'there is no God, and there never was'; it's a postmortem film.

Yet some, on some occasions including Polanski, have felt that the film derides all religion. In an interview, the director stated that: 'A point I am making is that people only dabble in superstition and Black Magic when they are disappointed by their own religions.'[35] The witches' religion is just another religion. When describing the witches, Rosemary consistently employs religious terms, making them cohere to the religion she knows: just as she's a 'martyr', the witches gather in a 'congregation', they conduct a 'sabbath'. The Satanism on display in the film parodies another religion, an impure overturning

of the Christianity it despises. Levin declared: 'My first note for
the book was, "an inversion of the Christ myth".'[36] Here Satanism
reverses the sacred, inverts the mass and reorders taste. The witches
prefer, or do not mind, putrid odours, unpleasant tastes; they would
rather smell devil's fungus than Revillon's Detchema. The disgusting
becomes, in Guy's words, 'not bad'. As part of its reversal of 'normal'
values, witchcraft here loves disgust; the witches eat horrible things,
they smell revolting, and, above all, look withered and unappealing
when nude. They are the dream figures of an archetypal aversion.

And Catholicism, contrariwise, becomes a parody of Satanism:
in the main dream sequence, Rosemary kisses the Pope's ring that
doubles as the tannis-root pendant given to her by Minnie. In these
ways, it is vital that the plot may be something dreamed up either by
a deluded Catholic or by those who wish to expose Catholicism as a
delusion.

The appalling plot that Rosemary possibly imagines may just
be the trace of her shallowly buried Catholic guilt. In the novel, we're
told that Rosemary's family are unhappy because she has married
a Protestant, in a registry office, and has a twice-divorced mother-
in-law, presently married to a Jew in Canada.[37] Moreover, Guy is
a modern agnostic Protestant, an actor, after all, in *Luther*, John
Osborne's psychologizing play on Martin Luther and the break with
the Roman Catholic church. However, Rosemary's Catholicism has
been put to one side, not forgotten or negated; Polanski denies that
Rosemary is 'lapsed'.[38] In addition to its symbolic resonances, the
plot requires that Rosemary be Catholic: abortion must be ruled
out as a solution to her predicament. 'I won't have an abortion,'
Rosemary asserts. (The landmark case of 'Roe v. Wade' was only a
year or so off from its inception.)

The film wants Rosemary to double with the Virgin Mary,
because that doubling is central to its shock tactics. Rosemary
imagines herself the mother of a dark messiah and ends the film in
blue and white – the Virgin Mary's colours.

Really, if the film were to be more thorough-going in its pursuit of a Christmas parody, Rosemary ought not to be a Roman Catholic, cornbread American, but Jewish. In many ways, the film's involvement in Jewish American culture (and Jewish culture beyond America) is as strong as its latent Catholicism. Levin, Castle, Evans and Sylbert were all New York Jews, and Polanski stands as a Jewish film-maker from a Catholic country. Curiously, Michael Shillo, the actor who played the Pope was also Jewish.

Jewishness acts as a strange presence here. It may tap into atavistic and scurrilous roots that link the Jew and the witch, even perhaps riffing on the old blood-libel stories of Jewish cannibalism and child sacrifice.[39] In particular, Dr Sapirstein embodies the mythic figure of the malevolent Jewish doctor; in the novel, Sapirstein is pointedly '"A Jewish man".'[40] Indeed, we may even read the film as one of Polanski's slantwise engagements with anti-Semitism and the Nazi persecutions and genocide. (At the party one of the guests remarks to the emaciated Rosemary, 'You look like Miss Concentration Camp '66'; *All of Them Witches* is published in 1933, the year Hitler took power.) Yet in the plot to give Satan a child there are also links to Nazism's yearning for the creation of a 'superman' figure – as played out in Levin's later novel, *The Boys From Brazil*.

A chalky undertaste

When, on the night planned for the conception, Minnie sends her chocolate mousse to Rosemary and Guy, it's one of several moments in which food assumes a place in a pattern of disgust. There's much food in the film, and on each occasion that it appears it's more nauseating and repellent than the last. During the film, we attend dinner with Hutch, we hear of the Trench sisters' cannibalism, we struggle through the ghastly dinner at the Castevets (Guy forces down two portions of Minnie's horrible dessert), we end a romantic meal with the chalky chocolate mousse, we catch Rosemary frying

her very rare steak, we spy on her chewing and gagging on raw offal. The pregnant woman's supposed yearnings for unusual and abhorrent food reaches an apogee there.

In an interview after *Rosemary's Baby's* release, Polanski is asked about how *Repulsion* shows his taste for potatoes and rabbits, and *Cul de Sac* for eggs, and the director interrupts and declares, 'that's not my taste, that's my disgust!'[41] Food repels and sickens in Polanski's early films, from the cannibal experiments in *Do You Like Women?* (1963) onwards.

The giving of food readily symbolizes the exchange of love. One of the guests at Rosemary's youthful party cheerfully warns her, 'you make him feed you, love'. But love here is suspect, unnourishing, its gifts apt to turn sickening. Rosemary grows thin, deprived of her own sustenance by the foetus within her. Pain suppresses appetite, and the fecundity that might be signalled in her pregnancy turns desiccated and lean. She herself becomes 'disgusting'; Guy will not touch her belly, won't even look at her. Rosemary does not bloom, she fades, and in the witches' inverted world that is how it should be; Minnie reassures Rosemary that after the birth, 'You'll be happy and thin again.'

The size of dreaming

The few spoons of mousse that Rosemary consumes, or the cocktails that precede the meal, leave her giddy. She reels and falls, and Guy carries her to her bed. She has lost control of herself, and Guy takes charge. And on the bed, she lapses back into a deeper loss of control. She enters her own dream, and the dream is here the great Gothic site for the loosening of the will and the expression of its imagined powerlessness.

In conceiving the film's three dream-sequences, Polanski began with the way that Rosemary's dreams are portrayed in Levin's novel. While following Levin's descriptions rather closely, Polanski brings to these moments a highly cinematic interest in subjectivity, and in the 'fluidity' of dreams, their quality as 'filmy' and insubstantial, the projected spectacle of an inner cinema. He remarks: 'One of the things I thought, that occurs in almost every dream, is that the fluidity of a dream, changes, it is the metamorphosis of things and people.'[42]

Identities are exchanged; the nun in Rosemary's first dream speaks with Minnie's voice. If what we are seeing is a dream, or wholly a dream, then we must take all the others we see here to be projections of Rosemary's own self, as well as her fantasies of others; the yacht they used for the longest dream was aptly named 'Alterego'. The first dream returns Rosemary to 'a composite of Our Lady's School, Uncle Mike's Body Shop and the candy counter in the Orpheum Cinema', all of which place the dreaming Rosemary as returning to childhood. The dream ends as 'Rosemary turns and she is at the candy counter with the other children.'[43] Adult self and childhood memories merge. In the second dream, spaces mingle: we move between the various dream locales and the sleepy site of the bedroom. The linen cupboard metamorphoses into the Sistine Chapel. The music too draws in another of Polanksi's films, the chords in the dream sequence/rape scene to my ear summoning up those used by Chico Hamilton in *Repulsion*, when the walls melt into mud under Carole's (Catherine Deneuve's) hands.

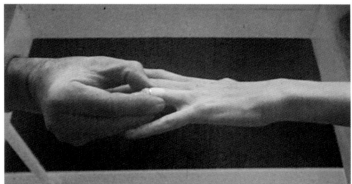

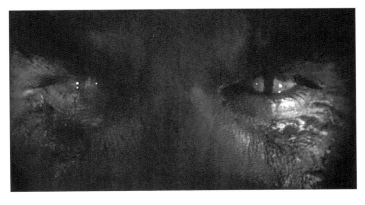

Undoubtedly, the cultural and personal impact of LSD informs these fugues. Just in the cultural moment when hallucinatory experience became increasingly central to the experience of youth, a drug releases Rosemary's central dream. When he came to make the movie, Polanski had taken LSD three times. In 1966, Polanski first took LSD, likely consuming a pill supplied by Michael Hollingshead, recently arrived from the USA, armed with acid and a few hundred copies of the Tibetan *Book of the Dead*.[44] The experience was a terrifying one, but he took it twice more, to more positive effect, with Sharon Tate. In the wider culture, such influences were, of course, widespread at the time; *Sgt. Pepper's Lonely Hearts Club Band* had come out at the beginning of June 1967, while the film was being prepared. William Castle's *The Tingler* had, ahead of the game, also employed a kind of LSD trip and stylized dream sequences. Stanley Kubrick's *2001, A Space Odyssey* came out in April 1968, with its famous Star Gate cosmic 'trip' similarly dismantling narrative coherence and rational cause and effect. The rational mind turns off; things stream and shift; psychedelic experience, dream and Gothic merge.

Rosemary's Baby is far from being a 'hippy' film, and the dispensers of hallucinogenics are countercultural geriatrics, yet the hippy moment flows through the movie. The acid experience was about the end of the stable ego, just as the art forms that embraced acid opted for the meandering and haphazard. The dream moments in *Rosemary's Baby* inject an appearance of looseness into a movie that is essentially structured.

The last dream, the one Rosemary has in the doctor's room, is a dream of security and American suburban happiness. Here there is no flux. There is instead the clarity of a distinct scene, one that is a fiction, although it believes itself, in its brief assurance, to be a prediction. A family gathers on a summer day to greet a new baby. Here people are themselves, siblings, relatives, friends. Although filtered through the gilded gauze of advertising images, it's the dream that most resembles 'real life' as we know it. It is also, in the world of this film, the least convincing, the least possible. For the movie is about to fall through its dream into a seminal scene of unremitting darkness.

With Tarquin's ravishing strides, towards his design

The rape at the centre of the film is the starkest way in which it performs its rites of control and subjugation. The movie's strongest scene of violence is a staged violence. That it takes place in what may or may not be a dream both renders it more bearable and adds a surreal force that intensifies its horror.

From *Repulsion* to *Tess*, rape has proved central to many of Polanski's movies.[45] His later occult movie, *The Ninth Gate* (1999) perhaps replays Rosemary's rape, with Green Eyes (Emmanuelle Seigner) as a demon (or angel) having sex with Johnny Depp, a consensual (male) reworking of the earlier scene as something chosen, though just as ambiguous an event as Rosemary's violation. Over and over, rape acts as an initiating transgression, an engine to narrative; in *Rosemary's Baby* it is the visible manifestation of an unseen contract. The critic Carol J. Clover once suggested that in a customary elision, repeated in so many classic Hollywood movies, Polanski's film cuts away from the sexual violence.[46] I do not see this; what is striking

and appalling in the film, is that it lingers over its defilement; it shows Rosemary in the moment of penetration and, if it does not persist until the Devil's orgasm, there must be few viewers who are not grateful for the scene's premature fading. We watch the rape; we do not witness the pact that permits it. In that off-screen bargain, it is Guy who is seduced.

The rape renders Rosemary vulnerable; it is the starkest instance of the plot's urge to enforce passivity upon her. Levin suggests that the rape takes 'only her body without her soul or self or she-ness – whatever it was [Guy] presumably loved'.[47] She becomes an object here, a means and not an end in herself. The extended scene paints a dark desacralization of the Annunciation, a moment of still calm where the original Mary embodies the apogee of consent.

Whatever else happens, a rape has definitely taken place; it is simply a question of who performed it. The victim of the rape is not in doubt; but who the perpetrator is seems an open question. Indeed, the movie turns on the question of who rapes Rosemary. A mystification about the actor who plays the Devil proves part of this confusion, with leading Satanist Anton LaVey falsely taking credit for the role. Some who have watched the film have imagined that the rapist is Guy in make-up.[48] In Polanski's script, the rapist is certainly not Satan but Guy 'wearing a suit of coarse leathery armour'.[49]

The moment evokes multiple forms of harm and transgression. Before the act, Guy pointedly removes Rosemary's wedding ring. Among its disturbances, if the rapist really is Satan, the scene evokes bestiality, the Devil who takes her being as much animal as person; in Levin's novel, during the act she feels that 'Guy's' penis is bigger than usual.[50] The Devil here is both less than and more than human, both beast and spirit; as Rosemary wonders, 'I dreamed someone was – raping me. I don't know – someone unhuman.' It seems vital to the movie's meanings that the Satan who rapes her should be so animalistic. This is no spiritual act of conception but something vile, purely physical, the manifestation of brute strength and will.

If the assailant is Satan, then the film revives a folkloric archetype of the demon lover, a fair maiden abducted by an infernal spirit – though in such stories the demon is a seducer gifted in the arts of persuasion, not a wordless brute. Sir Walter Scott writes of the notion 'that the ancestor of the English monarchs, Geoffrey Plantagenet, had actually married a demon'.[51] Merlin too was supposedly born of a demon father and human mother, and *The Tempest's* Caliban is half-human, half-devil. The mythic element here concerns the intermingling of the human and the unhuman, and the conception of a new kind of creature, partaking of two natures, a fairy lover, a malign machine (as in *Demon Seed* [1977]), an alien, as in *The Midwich Cuckoos* [1957]). (In a 1969 interview Polanski praised the latter's film adaptation, *Village of the Damned* [1960].)[52]

If the rapist is Guy, who has sex with her while she is unconscious, then what even he names his 'necrophiliac' desire evidences extreme aggression. Such an act empties out a person into a sex object. In some ways, this is the less repellent of the two options with which the film presents us. It is the 'realistic' resolution to the scene's palpable distress. And yet, how fearful, how vile is their relationship, when this marital assault seems the lesser evil.

The scene rightly disturbs us. There is almost nothing in it that is redemptive or that might assuage the abuse it records. In Polanski's script, Rosemary does not take a shower; her doing so in the movie itself offers an attenuated act of self-care. The witches and Guy have done something that might be seen as defiling Rosemary. Nonetheless, she remains herself, 'a specific person and not just an object in a game', someone 'living, delicate, and loved'.[53]

On her waking, viewers now may lose patience with Rosemary as a victim, her shrugging acceptance of the marital rape making her too passive. Rosemary's ordeal is to suffer. In the novel, Rosemary has a counter-plot against Guy: her aim is to get pregnant, whether he wants it or not. Significantly, Polanski drops this aspect of the story, making Rosemary both more sympathetic and more helpless. Her passivity finds echoes throughout the film: in the comas entered into by Mrs Gardenia, the apartment's previous tenant, and by Hutch, as in the reiterated scenes of sleeping and dreaming. If Rosemary retains agency in this long scene, she does so only in the sense that the event happens in, and is mediated through, her dream. This dreamed version of reality, or this mere dream (depending on how you interpret it) belongs to her, it is a film she makes, either something inflicted by others or by her 'subconscious'. The only agency on offer here is the agency of virtuous docility or of masochism.

This is really happening

At the rape scene's end, Rosemary protests, 'This is no dream, this is really happening!' As a statement made in the artifice of a film, this is intriguing; but what it connects to in the real world is unbearable. Here dreaming negates itself, though it does so in the dream. When Rosemary awakes, she no longer holds onto the epiphany that the dream gave her. Even when she sees through the witches' plot, she still cannot see what the audience saw, that Satan is her baby's father.

If we watch films as if they are really happening, what happens then in scenes of violence, of rape? We may fight back our distress at the distress of others by saying, no, this is not really happening, this is a dream, a film. Do we then let ourselves off the hook? The dream lulls us, the music hypnotizes us with its surge and sway, and like Rosemary we are rocked to sleep. If we feel that things are real, as Rosemary tells us they are, we suffer with her, we are also tortured, also trapped. Only if we remember it is art, can we step back, disengaged and impervious.

On the DVD commentary to *Repulsion*, Polanski states, 'A film should be presented as a book written in the first person.' Polanski was particularly impressed by R.L. Gregory's *Eye and Brain: The Psychology of Seeing* (1966), which he believed 'lent scientific confirmation to many of the ideas I'd instinctively believed in since my film-school days – for instance, on the subject of perspective, size constancy, and optical illusions'.[54]

With rare exceptions, such as her receiving news of Hutch's death, nearly every shot involves Rosemary's perspective: 'I chose the camera angles thinking of Rosemary, and trying to convey, more or less, her perception of events.'[55] Polanski and Fraker shot the film in such a way that the audience struggled to see things more clearly, with characters sometimes almost out of shot, so as to reproduce what Rosemary herself would be able to see: 'Much of the film is seen through Rosemary's eyes. In trying to convey this subjective immediacy, I often staged long, complicated scenes using short focal lenses that called for extreme precision in the placing of both camera and actors … Ideally, the lens should be at the same distance from the subject as the eye of the notional observer.'[56]

A strong sense of seeing what Rosemary sees occurs most often when people are on the phone, or as when, while washing-up with Minnie, Rosemary sees the cigar smoke drifting from Guy and Roman's conversation. Perhaps we are not fully and consistently inside Rosemary's point of view, but certainly we watch her, we are involved through her involvement in the plot. Technique fosters this attachment. The film's use of a wide-angle lens foregrounds Rosemary and anchors us to her point of view, while creating depth around her.[57]

When Rosemary divines that her child has something wrong
with his eyes ('what have you done to his eyes!'), she picks up one
ongoing theme in the film, which acknowledges its own voyeurism
and shows a Hitchcockian concern with gazing, with point of view
and with the eye itself. Three times in the film, our eyes are opened
to what someone sees with their inner eye in the internal space of
dreams. A person may be glimpsed within the eye, though eyes
themselves are avoided in the film ('why do you never look at me?')
or become hideous, bestial, conduits for hostility or strangeness.
Satan looks Rosemary, and us, in the eyes.

In any case, questions of point of view dominate the way we
respond to the film. It can seem a textbook example of the uncanny,
the mode in which fear arises from an essential hesitation in our
ability unequivocally to interpret what we see. After all, is Rosemary
mad or the victim of a devilish conspiracy? Polanski frames a film
poised between doubt and faith, passing from one to the other; we
believe with Rosemary or we doubt her with Guy.

With the movie conflicting with Polanski's rational view of
the world, choosing the uncanny was a way of saving face: 'For
credibility's sake, I decided that there would have to be a loophole –
the possibility that Rosemary's supernatural experiences were
figments of her imagination.'[58] As Penelope Houston put it: 'The
trick of this freezing little story is to persuade its audience that it
would rather have Rosemary sane (in which case practically everyone
around her must be rationally accepted as an active black-magicking
practitioner) than have her mad (in which case she's merely doing a
lot of fantasy damage to herself).'[59]

Polanski's autobiography commences by playing with these
matters: 'For as far back as I can remember, the line between fantasy
and reality has been hopelessly blurred.'[60] It's a mischievous opening,
an outrageous joke to play at the opening of what purports to be a
non-fiction book, telling us from the start that a memoir (especially
one called *Roman*, the French for a novel) is necessarily also a work
of fiction – a construction of events and not the truth. This same

artfulness pervades the film too. Polanski declared that his primary intention was to make sure the audience were not sure what was going on, that we should be uncertain.[61]

This was Polanski's interest, not Levin's. Levin wanted the rape to be an actual rape by the Devil: 'I was writing a thriller, and it believed it absolutely. Subsequently, I received letters from psychiatrists who said, well, obviously it was a delusion, wasn't it? I said no. And they said, this was postpartum depression, right? And I said no, no, it's very real.'[62]

One obvious thing militating against the madness theory is simply that Rosemary does not come across as mentally ill. She's depressed perhaps, and with good reason, but nevertheless she's strongly rational, reasonably anxious. This is more than just a result of our sharing her point of view so strongly, it's really a consequence of her affect. 'You're in Dubrovnik, I don't hear you,' says Rosemary, as, like us, she sees the supposedly globe-trotting Roman there in his apartment; the sarcasm hardly suggests insanity.

Rosemary's Baby does not reflect the world, it reflects the human mind – but not only the rational, perceiving mind but the haunted self, the dreaming self. It plays out in the fugitive shadow realm. After all, film is already always a dream, a complex perception that makes a world. The movie has the continuity, the flow, of a dream, and yet like a dream it proves subject to sudden disruptions, to the abrupt shift, the shattering turn, though these too follow a dream logic of events. The cinema of the fantastic challenges 'natural perception'; it records the everyday world but shows that world as extraordinary, gripped by the possibility of astonishment. The 1960s predilection for absurdity and irrationality pervades the film. The dreamer in the cinema seat belongs to Rosemary's predicament, disconcertingly unable to sort out the status of what is seen.

Our proneness to perceive forms and make patterns belongs to an intrinsic capacity of the mind to look constantly for new interpretations. Watching a film, the brain unstably moves on, taking things in as it goes. A 'constant drift' characterizes the process of film and *Rosemary's Baby* in particular. For, after all, 'drift' lies at the heart of 1960s films, given over to a rhythm that wants to embrace purposeless waiting, recumbent in the pool in *The Graduate*, on the road in *Easy Rider* (1969), lost at the party in all those Antonioni films, loose in those places of play in early Godard. Set against the drift rises the incursive urgency of plot – wanting to marry Elaine, robbing a house, being persecuted by witches. Rosemary's problem is that her plot seems imposed on her. Her activity consists in perceiving the full extent of her passivity.

The film invites us to question the imagination as such, including the darkness of what we imagine when we imagine a story such as *Rosemary's Baby*. Through its wavering commitment to the uncanny, the film enacts a basic property of the mind, that is, the way in which the mind never rests or stabilizes, but constantly moves, hunting links and connections, seeking patterns. Rosemary's quest to locate meaning parallels the audience's. Her work proves identical with that of the critics (aware of all those contextual connections, stretching before the film and after and all around it, weaving a web). The movie prompts and then frustrates the mind's innate scepticism. We do not want the world our mind restlessly, relentlessly presents to us; we want finality, rest. We want the voice in our head to stop.

The pregnant pause

One strand of criticism on the film rightly sees it as an instance of the gynaecological Gothic (in Penelope Gilliatt's phrase).[63] In this connection, the film taps into worry about pregnancy as well as fears regarding such things as the Thalidomide scandal. (In the novel, Levin references Thalidomide anxiety, saying how Rosemary wishes to avoid 'great new drugs with Thalidomide side effects'.)[64]

These fears of a constrained feminine body and a damaged vulnerable unborn child are at once absolutely contemporary and radically atavistic. It is fundamental to how *Rosemary's Baby* works that these current anxieties should return us, in the manner of Gothic, to ancient terrors.

As is hardly unique, Rosemary's pregnancy sickens her. Farrow performs pregnancy here, doing so with admirable accuracy. She observed pregnant women, endeavouring to reproduce a pregnant woman's rolling, flat-footed gait.[65] How many films make any kind of reference to their protagonist's menstrual cycle? Terry's 'depression' (as described by Roman) occurs every three weeks; Rosemary too becomes ill and depressed on the first day of her period; Laura-Louise laments her menstrual pain – though in her case, it's a thing of the past.

If pregnancy is an illness, then naturally enough it becomes the province of doctors. In a movie that turns on the compromise of the will, medical supervision becomes a mode of control, another way to penetrate and constrict the body. There are three injections in the film, plus one more that is supposed to be given (another blood test), and numerous pills and tablets and vitamin drinks ingested or refused. In the novel, Rosemary desires a natural childbirth and a natural rearing ('Definitely. Breast-fed, not bottle-fed'); she gets neither: 'This wasn't Natural Childbirth, at all; she wasn't helping, she wasn't seeing.'[66] It's Rosemary's baby, and yet almost everyone else takes charge of her pregnancy – planned by her husband (he's ringed the best dates for a conception on the calendar), watched over by the neighbours, directed by doctors. It is Guy, 'not Rosemary, [who] knows that she is exactly two days overdue'.[67] Equally intrusive, Minnie Castevet haunts the film as the modern version (hidden and despised) of the 'midwife-witch'.[68] However, the supervising force, the villain of the pregnancy is Dr Sapirstein. He plays much the same role as a Satanist vicar would in a British version of the hidden coven story: that is, he's defined as a comforter by his social role, as someone who *ought* not to be a witch.

In watching the film, it is, I believe, impossible to identify with the foetus or later with the baby. We rarely share Rosemary's overwhelming anxiety for its safety. Rather, as Levin intended, we fear, as Rosemary does not, the baby itself. The 'It's alive' speech given at the close of the party with her young friends references James Whale's *Frankenstein* (1931), a sign that the birth will be a monstrous one. Rosemary's joy is our anxiety. Though it may be a blindness in us, we don't wish to pray for Rosemary's baby, we'd rather pray for Rosemary. This is of a piece with a tendency in responses to the film to see the child as fundamentally the Devil's offspring, not (despite the film's title) hers. The foetus is an alien invader, another version of the demonic rapist who fathered it. He has his father's eyes.

Levin enjoyed the fact that the pregnancy creates a nine-month-long period of suspense. As soon as you're pregnant, the clock starts ticking and birth is inevitable. Polanski remarked: 'What attracted me to *Rosemary* was the suspense.'[69] Time passes, and throughout the movie clocks tick, marking the moments' passing. The presence of those ticking clocks makes for an oppressive, enchanted stillness, the baby itself being a nine-month time-bomb heading for detonation.

The passing of the seasons is vital to the film, which moves from one summer, through fall, and goes through winter back into another sweltering New York summer. The movie is a time-piece. Rosemary wishes that it would be the coldest winter for eighty years, which is ever since Steven Marcato was born. Few films are so obsessive, or so accurate, in relation to the calendar. It plays in relation to real dates, a background documentary context of the real world to set against the Gothic fantasy, with Guy's precise theatrical CV, the Pope's visit, the 8 April 1966 cover of *Time*. The film itself opens on 1 August 1965. The dinner at Hutch's apartment takes place on 5 August. They move in and make love in the empty apartment on 20 August. Rosemary meets Terry in the basement laundry room on 10 September 1965; exactly one week later, Terry dies. On 20 September comes the dinner at the Castevets; the next night Rosemary hopes to spend alone with a book. It's the first day of her period; she'll be most fertile in two weeks' time. Sure enough, the night of the conception is 4 October 1965. On 22 October, her period is due; on 30 October, she hears from Dr Hill that she is pregnant, and the due date is 28 June. Appropriately enough, her visit to Dr Sapirstein comes on Halloween, 1965; Minnie gives Rosemary her first vitamin drink on All Saints' Day, the day she was due to have her second blood test with Dr Hill. On 21 November, Rosemary visits Vidal Sassoon for a haircut. On 10 December 1965, she goes to meet Hutch at the Time-Life Building. New Year's Eve follows, and the toast to 1966, 'The Year One.' The party for Rosemary's young friends takes place on Saturday, 22 January 1966. The film then cuts to 15 April and preparing the nursery room, and then to 7 June 1966, and the news of the death of Hutch. The birth comes on 25 June 1966 (25.6.66).

Pregnancy too is a narrative, one that provides its own end-point. It holds us to a period of waiting that must end – though uncertainty disquietens the sense of what that end will be. Birth itself becomes Gothic; it is terrifying, uncertain, a giving of life that is also potentially murderous. Something strange occupies the body in a kind of possession. In relation to the film, Jenny Diski once wrote: 'Pregnancy is the state in which women are most alien to men. This is not unreasonable: it's also the state in which they may be most alien to themselves.'[70] Perhaps the man's fear (Polanski's fear at the time) is that having a baby is an emasculation, a clog. The baby seems the woman's possession and a way of more fully possessing the man who fathers it. In fact, in this film the baby instead disempowers Rosemary and evidences Guy's dominance.

Rosemary and Guy choose to try to become parents. Yet the conception itself takes place without being chosen by Rosemary; it's no choice, but a choice overthrown, one perverted into a coercion. From then on, pregnancy is a choice that leads to an absence of choice. The only choice left (which Rosemary will not take) is the choice of abortion. It resembles the inevitability of death; necessity, not freedom is its essence. It therefore challenges our understanding of the human subject as defined by free will. No *acte gratuit* is possible to the pregnant woman after the first voluntary decision. Your pregnancy happens to you; the baby comes in its time, not yours. Rosemary's body becomes her own enemy, a place where evil bides its time. At the end, the contractions will end her flight from the 'safety' of the flat. The person experiences the limitations of the self in relation to 'nature'. This biological determinism confronts a culture that regrets all such limitations. Even Rosemary's supposed madness is deemed merely hormonal, a set of behaviours and not an act or an individual response.

Yet at the centre of this process is a person, with desires, wishes, a history. This most natural of processes is, with death itself, one of the places where our distance from the life of beasts is most apparent. Constrained by nature, we are not limited to it. Merely to be a human being in biological terms entails a potential loss of self. It marks a crisis in the life of the subject, which seems not free but constrained. The conception also depends on another who becomes suspect, a Guy who may be a Satan. At the end of the movie, Rosemary cries out, 'what have you done to its eyes'. Polanski has suggested that when she says this we've been seeing Guy's shifty eyes, and the line could therefore refer to them.[71] In another sense, they might be Guy's eyes by the laws of heredity. What if they are, genetically speaking, Guy's eyes; might not that be trauma enough?

The anaesthetized woman

Rather often, *Rosemary's Baby's* reviewers assumed that it is a film both peculiarly aimed at women, and yet also designed to upset and unnerve them.[72] It has seemed both a woman's film and a misogynist's film, a paradox central to the debates on Polanski's oeuvre. Molly Haskell berated him for his preference for the woman as 'murderous somnambulist'. Was his treatment of women an act of exploitation or an exposé of the way in which modern Western society degrades women? Haskell feared it was the former: 'Polanski is a perfect example of the artist whose vision of women is not formed according to what he sees, but conversely, whose women are chosen [she calls them 'lobotomised'] to conform to his preconceptions.'[73]

Others, most eloquently Jenny Diski, have suggested that ambiguity is central to his treatment of women, which can veer from puerile pornography to 'moments of remarkable sensitivity', running the range from disgust to empathy.[74] More or less voicing the problem, Polanski has asserted: 'I've always preferred the central protagonists of my films to be female, and [...] I generally like female characters who are victims.'[75] (He has discussed his belief that in movies women make the best victims, as they are more easily frightened than men; though crucially he goes on to say that 'the reactions of the one who frightens and the one who is being frightened, they actually resemble each other', and what might be bullying sexism becomes a strange sympathy.)[76] His forte is 'la femme prisonnière'.[77] He has further suggested that he has made women's films from time to time, even perhaps feminist films.[78]

As *Season of the Witch* (1972) and *The Witches of Eastwick* (1987) show, to talk about witches is to talk of women's powerlessness and power; the expression of male anxieties about the feminist revolution imbue these films. In this regard, the previous tenant of Rosemary's flat, Mrs Gardenia, acts as a strange double for Rosemary. She stands both as a witch and the witches' victim. Unlike Rosemary, whose 'career' is to be a housewife and mother, Mrs Gardenia was one of the first woman lawyers in New York – an admirably go-getting figure from the first wave of feminism.

Most curious, I would argue, is our suspicion that as the film identifies mostly with Rosemary, so does Polanski. On the commentary for *Repulsion*, Deneuve has spoken of Polanski's romantic feelings for young, naive, 'pure' girls (as evidenced in the feeling for Carole in *Repulsion*, for Sharon Tate's character in *Fearless Vampire Killers*, for Rosemary, for Thomas Hardy's Tess). She goes on to say that one reason that Polanski made *The Tenant* (1976) was to *be* Carole from *Repulsion*. Indeed, Polanski has shown himself apt to play the woman's part, becoming the old woman in *When Angels Fall* or turning himself into the previous female tenant in *The Tenant* (not to mention the cross-dressing in *Cul De Sac*). Likewise, his directing style involved enacting the role for the actors, so that he played out Rosemary to Farrow to show her how he wanted the part performed. The script to *Rosemary's Baby* tells us that the last dream in the film, when she believes she's safe at Dr Hill's, takes place in Beverly Hills. In other words, newly resident there with Tate, the reference here is as much to Polanski's future, as to Rosemary's own.[79] His putting himself in the woman's shoes may inform the fact that, unlike Stanley Kubrick palling up with Jack Nicholson and bullying Shelley Duvall while making *The Shining* (1980), during the shooting Polanski was friends with Farrow and fought Cassavetes.

This process of empathy returns us to the movie's preoccupation with point of view and its Gothic insistence on having us share the persecutions of a woman victim. Much depends on how sympathetically we view Rosemary. In an interview, film director Peter Yates remarked of Farrow's performance in *John and Mary* (1969) – 'She is original; she is inquisitive; she is very likeable, which is very much a change of part from *Rosemary's Baby* for Mia.'[80] I would say that Farrow is already original, inquisitive and likeable in Polanski's film. We suffer and struggle with her. If the movie is interested in creating unsympathetic others, then those others would be Guy, the old, and the ambiguous figure of the witch.

Five to one, one in five

In *Rosemary's Baby*, we attend two parties. The first, a sedate New Year's affair, takes place at Roman and Minnie's apartment, where elderly people converse quietly, drinks in their hands.[81] The second turns out to be a very special party: 'you have to be under sixty to get in'. It is a striking feature of the film that for the most part the witches are old-age pensioners. For plot reasons, the witches are old so that no one in the coven can bear children; they require a young outsider – not a recruit though, or an adept, but a victim. More vitally, at the height of protests against the war in Vietnam, *Rosemary's Baby* advises us that the young should fear and avoid the old. These witches may see themselves as the oppressed but in political terms they are the oppressors, the generation who backed Vietnam and not those who were dying there.

Polanski has declared that: 'Old people fascinated me. I'd always felt that the old were even more deserving of care and attention than the young. They were so helpless, so resigned, so ignorant of life despite their accumulated experience and proximity to death.'[82] In *Rosemary's Baby*, the old are far from contemptible. Criminal and occult, the old initiate the project; an absurd hopefulness pulses through their machinations. It is something in your eighties still to be enacting schemes to conquer the world.

In his review, Alexander Walker remarked on the film's exploitation of the 'generation gap'.[83] To Frank Sinatra and his

generation, Farrow's Vidal Sassoon haircut was already a symbol of youthful modernity. Farrow was a hippy married to a Rat Pack crooner; her public persona both pointed to the conflict between youth and age and suggested that some kind of reconciliation might be possible, 'linking the Establishment and youth culture, the studio system and New American cinema'.[84] The film itself could seem a meeting place for old and new Hollywoods: the pressbook for the movie stressed that it was a mix of young and old, with Ira Levin, Polanski, Farrow, Cassavetes working together with Castle, Gordon, Blackmer and Maurice Evans.

Yet the fact of the Vietnam War meant that young and old were set against each other, the baby boomer generation rejecting the values and commitments of the old. The witches are a strange mixture of both sides, being countercultural subversives who are simultaneously exemplars of the old guard, conservatives ('the old ways are back') willing to impose their authority on the young. More usually, James Leo Herlihy's *Season of the Witch* allies the occult with the hippy movement; George Romero's film of that novel shows witchcraft as a way of (sexually) liberating the dull bourgeois self. In *Rosemary's Baby*, the witch *is* the dull bourgeois self. In the novel and script, when Laura-Louise comes to visit, she has 'a Buckley-for-Mayor button on the shoulder of her green dress', and in 1965 one could hardly get more conservative than that.

At the Cannes Film Festival in May 1968, Polanski showed himself a sceptic when it came to the revolutionary impulses of the moment, and his film can appear to be outside the political currents and connections of that year; in fact, here too its apparent Gothic confinement is porous. Political fears break in, reaching into the debates on race and civil rights. In Rosemary's central dream, the subservient uniformed African American elevator-operator becomes a threatening, commanding ship's mate, sternly ordering Rosemary to get below. Relations that might provoke anxiety in Rosemary's white consciousness reappear here in dreams, and it is precisely as a dream of oppression that the film expresses its power.

The name is an anagram

Readings of *Rosemary's Baby* have often assumed that it seems to belong within a web of contexts and correspondences. I share this belief, while also wondering what it is about this film that invites such interpretations. In this movie, meaning is always deferred, always elsewhere. This is a film whose significance appears to be hidden, a matter of puzzles and unexpected connections. In the era of *The Manchurian Candidate* (1962) and Thomas Pynchon's *The Crying of Lot 49* (1966), of the Warren Report and Sirhan Sirhan, it plays out paranoia. Both book and film are laced with references to the Kennedys: in her dreams, Rosemary meets her fellow Catholics, the Pope, and John and Jackie Kennedy; in the script, when Roman leaves for Dubrovnik, his parting line is 'Kennedy Airport. TWA building'.[85] In novel and script these links were even more pointed: Polanski has Roman Castevet discussing Kennedy's assassination ('Do *you* think it could have been a plot of some kind?'); Levin has the head witch reading 'a book critical of the Warren Report, about the Kennedy assassination'.[86]

Rosemary's Baby takes its place as a key exemplar of the new paranoia and anxiety about conspiracy, an especially 1960s concern that continues to resonate in our own surveyed and manipulated lives.

Conspiracy and the supernatural had long been interconnected, all the way back to the sources for *Macbeth* (Polanski's next film), the Bothwell Conspiracy and the Gowrie Conspiracy. In Shakespeare's day, witches and assassins seemed allied. In *Rosemary's Baby*, Gothic and conspiracy come together and form a highly disturbing merger.

Rosemary's Baby is a paranoid fiction, characterized by a mood of disquiet, the sense that nothing is as we perceive it. Conspiracy theories are for the 'clear-seeing' minority, the supposedly undeceived. They offer a dream of self-importance, the paranoid justifying their existence on the basis that they have such splendid enemies. In our culture, the great figure of 'knowing' is the detective, and the paranoid fiction is a close cousin of the detective story, though it lacks the latter's rational and comforting quality.

The job of the detective figure is to link together apparently random elements within the film; to connect the dots, to follow the money. Rosemary, our detective, sees what others miss: the taken-down pictures; the pierced ears; Guy knowing that Mr Shand plays the flute. The movie subtly places clues and plot-points, calling on us to recall moments from the film and reinterpret them. Rosemary's sense of who is in on the conspiracy keeps expanding; it begins with Roman and Minnie, then focuses on Guy, and, finally, Dr Sapirstein.

For the classic detective tale, the solution shrinks the story, pinning all the possible guilt on one suspect. In the paranoid fiction, solving the crime does not establish peace. Rosemary learns the truth, but it brings ultimate distress and not consolation. The exposed mystery is so immense that it deluges our detective Rosemary, overwhelming all possibility of resolution; corruption ramifies endlessly. You unravel a conspiracy, reconstruct its plot; you cannot 'solve' it.

Conspiracy films proffer grim pleasures. In the guise of exposing secrets, they are as often dissolving the real. So it is that such films show us things that rationally speaking cannot be there – the Devil's lascivious presence held in a Manhattan apartment. Reality becomes suspect; the surface must be continually reassessed. In all conspiracy films, the accepted world of the ordinary may turn out to be extraordinary, but only in the sense of being extraordinarily dark. Things are far worse than you believed. Either you are mad to credit the conspiracy, or the world is mad to have allowed it. In *The Stepford Wives* (1975), as she considers her suspicions about what's going on in Stepford, Katharine Ross agonizes, much as Rosemary might have, 'It's so awful. If I'm wrong, I'm insane. And if I'm right, it's worse than if I'm wrong.'

Rosemary's private pregnancy, her sex life, her fertility, all become public property. Other people are concerned in it. In this, Rosemary's world lapses back to an earlier model of the public/private space, where marriage and birth are possessions of all. In New York, she finds herself in a gossips' village. Someone watches her every move; her privacy erodes and vanishes. Minnie winkles out information, spying and gaining knowledge while appearing as if she's not really listening to the answers. Here there can be no secrets. Others must be constantly updated; there's no room for her, for her private concerns, other than the space mediated by the neighbours, the witches. She may tentatively confess her anxiety to Hutch, but after his death she exists without a confidant. She finds herself alone with no one to trust. Increasingly she talks to herself, her only addressee, and in the process, she speaks to us in the audience.

We have come to suspect the stories we are told, to doubt the evidence of our eyes. The great fear is manipulation – by the government, by corporations, by criminals, and, finally, by film itself. Curiously, we believe in the witches long before Rosemary does – in the Scrabble scene, she's not discovering some secret we have not guessed, she's catching up with our knowledge – at last knowing what we know. Indeed, Rosemary dismisses Hutch's warnings about the Bramford on the basis that all such apartment buildings must have similar histories, an oddly naive investment in the certainty of the ubiquity of wickedness. At first, she's an innocent, troubled by evil, but not believing in it – until (in the end) she believes in nothing else. Her path to knowing is a frustratingly slow one.

In grasping the conspiracy against her, Rosemary refuses its power. She asserts her right to unravel her own story. It's a story of control, but Hutch's message shows that an absolute control is hard to organize; word gets through. Given the film's religious preoccupations, it is noteworthy that the message comes via 'Grace' Cardiff.

Rosemary falls into perceiving the people around her as evil. All of them are witches. Her fantasy is less unique than might be thought. There's the case of the paranoid Carl Walters, in Tennessee in 1950, who shot dead Alberta Gibbons and her mother, Alta Woods – because 'I was tired of being bewitched.'[87] There are other such incidents throughout the 1950s, most often related to Hispanic or African American culture or to poor whites. Rosemary is a middle-class victim, in a culture where the bourgeois are not meant to suffer such things or to believe them, either.

In the 1950s and 1960s, more usually the objects of suspicion were no longer witches but rather communists, aliens, or the industrial-military complex behind the government. Suspicions regarding witchcraft ceased to be a community fear and became an individual one, something you were likely to feel disinclined to share with others, lest you seem crazy. Both Gothic and conspiracy evoke the question of credibility. What and whom do we believe are central to their meanings. The terror of *Rosemary's Baby* is in part the terror of being controlled and in part of not being listened to, of your words not counting. When Dr Hill appears to doubt Rosemary's story, we know that's fair enough, and that in a similar situation, we also would doubt: 'But at this point the audience hopes urgently for Dr. Hill's belief. The audience thus urges belief in witchcraft – a thing which its entire culture calls unbelievable these days.'[88] Above all, the believer in conspiracy longs for the confirmation that another person believes too, both in the plot and therefore in them.

The movie proceeds slowly (its average shot length around the 16 second mark – the median shot length around 8 seconds, the same more or less as *Chinatown* [1974]). Suspense finds itself in the discovery of the very plot that shapes the film. Thereafter, tension comes through the hope that someone else might be found who can share the secret, or that Rosemary might escape the premise of the film that contains her.

In a world where God is dead, the basis of authority collapses and mere power rules. This, after all, is a film whose subject is power. Authority's absence does not just create a world based on power, it creates a world based on the surface of the image – whether that of advertising, of fashion or of film itself. Here the person becomes something imaged and consumed. So it is that Rosemary proves ripe for consumption, an object in a transaction, the price of a deal and hence deprived of value in herself.

In the age of paranoia, the anxieties expressed in Rosemary are found everywhere; with the similarly pregnant heroine of John Bowen's excellent BBC play, *Robin Redbreast* (1970), just as with Edward Woodward's entrapped puritan policeman in Anthony Shaffer's *The Wicker Man* (1973). Gothic requires victims and, above all, inexplicably semi-willing ones; it is not just being taken over that provides the terror but our knowledge of our collusion in the process, our inner compulsion to give ourselves over to desire or death. Gothic tenders us a permeable self, susceptible to invasion, where our subconscious mind is our private Fifth Column. In vampire films, the 'victim' is a kind of addict, consciously repelled, unconsciously attracted. Rosemary would resist her rape, but for much of the film weakly colludes in the oppression meted out by her doctor, her neighbours and her husband. Through the best Gothic stories, sleep-walkers, the mesmerized, the entranced and enchanted stalk. The 1960s and 1970s could connect such radical absence of will to mind control, propaganda and the hidden persuasion of advertising; with brainwashing, the world had gone Gothic.

In conspiracy theory, everything connects with everything else. The critic Lucy Fischer has described the 'space' of *Rosemary's Baby* as opening out into other contiguous spaces, coming into touch with a myriad of contexts and discourses.[89] I trace some of them here – food, Vietnam, the Kennedys, Thalidomide, occultism – but, in fact, the contexts are endless. The film invites us to catch meaning circulating among its network of references, but that meaning never arrives, it is only postponed, reconnected. Facts shimmer and reposition themselves. In watching the film, we share Rosemary's paranoia; we are involved in it. Who knows where the plot's, the movie's ramifications will end? The film derives from a moment in American life when, with the influence of post-structuralism, to some there appeared to be no truths of any kind. 'Truth' was only a social construct, a necessary fiction. Similarly, the emerging New Age moment manifested a suspicion of reason and science, preferring coincidence. If truths are present, then they are concealed and only exist as part of a web, where meaning is dispersed and interconnected, neither whole or graspable in itself.

The devil of fashion
Chief among this web of connections is the link to Satanism. In an obvious sense, *Rosemary's Baby* concerns witches; yet the movie itself shows a peculiar lack of interest in them. It's striking how little the film expresses concern regarding what the witches actually believe. All we know is what they do, in public, and, at the end, that they are antagonistic towards Christianity and prepared to harm

people to get what they want. One reason for this lacuna is that the film is not about their beliefs, it is about ours, and more especially about Rosemary's. In this way, the witches are merely cyphers for a malevolence inexplicably directed towards the self.

The only people on the team who seem to have actively researched the occult were Dick and Anthea Sylbert. They explored 'the iconography and mythology of the devil and witchcraft, going back to medieval etchings, Dick Sylbert mostly applied this newfound knowledge to the dream sequence and the props such as the tannis-root charm and books about witches'.[90] Polanski declared that he had not bothered to do much investigation of witchcraft (only 'très peu'). However, two years before making the film he had been introduced to a king and queen witch on a TV show. (They suggested that Polanski had enough sympathy to be a witch.) In any case, in his view *Rosemary's Baby* was not a film about witches.[91] In saying that I do not think Polanski was being disingenuous. Nearly always in talking about the film, it is the technical aspect that engages him, while the theme embarrasses him. His primary interest was in creating a well-made film and in telling, as effectively as possible, a story. The film was meant to be fun. '*Rosemary's Baby* is the perfect thriller to me. And it has sobriety. The older I am, the more

I understand that simplicity is the most important, and most difficult, thing.'[92] He asserted that: 'When it comes to cinema, evil is simply a form of entertainment to me.'[93]

The film might not really concern contemporary Satanism at all, or only offers a cartoon version of it. Yet it remains the case that the witchcraft presented in *Rosemary's Baby* belongs to a specifically late 1960s cultural moment, in which the occult became both an object of anxious titillation and one focus of a diffuse interest in the irrational, the transgressive and the individualistic. In 1966, Eric Maple published *The Domain of Devils*, a sensationalist journalistic exposé of the influence of Satan in history lurid enough to influence Levin. But the image of the witch was anyway ubiquitous just then. In 1964, the TV sitcom *Bewitched* first aired – a gentle suburban version of *I Married A Witch* (1942) or the 1958 Kim Novak vehicle, *Bell, Book and Candle* – turning witchcraft into a comedy of the sexes. That same year another ABC show, *The Addams Family* appeared, a comic Gothic version of the nuclear family. In 1968, Louise Huebner became 'Official Witch of Los Angeles County' and gave a series of summer concerts at the Hollywood Bowl; TV chat shows were boosting the fame of British witch, Sybil Leek. The film plays in the light of *Their Satanic Majesties* and *The Devil Rides Out*, of Aleister Crowley on the cover of *Sgt. Pepper*, of the Process Church and Charles Manson, of Anton LaVey and Kenneth Anger.

For a long time, *Rosemary's Baby* was erroneously linked to Anton LaVey, the theatrical and compelling leader of the Los Angeles-based Church of Satan. He was reputed to be, but was not, Polanski's 'technical advisor'. Born in Chicago in 1930 as Howard Stanton Levey, LaVey was a gifted showman, self-mythologizer and performer, given to wandering the Bay Area with his pet lion, Togare. Here was someone with the chutzpah and talent to make transgression trendy. LaVey initiated the Church of Satan on Walpurgisnacht, 1966, and, as Roman Castevet does, declared in the process, the Year One. Belief in an actual fallen angel named Satan was never central to LaVey's movement, which was more interested in Ayn Rand than the *Malleus*

Maleficarum. The Church of Satan also had few connections to the post-war Wiccan movement, with the latter really being a neo-pagan movement.[94] With social Darwinism central to his thinking, LaVey's view was that the human was an animal fallen from beasthood. Pretending to have played the Devil's part in the film, LaVey describes Rosemary's rape as the bestial in man in ritualized form reawakening the virginal mind with its own animalism. There is only the ego and its desires, which must be achieved through strength and force of will. Control was the key, and everything, including irrational forces, that gave control was a good. Humility and meekness are weaknesses and those who possess them deserve to be crushed. In *Rosemary's Baby*, if individualism and selfishness are the criteria, then the truest Satanist is Guy. The pitiless character of LaVey's Satanism becomes apparent from the way he reads Terry Gionoffrio's suicide/murder. As far as he sees it, she dies because she is a loser – a drug-addict, a potential bad mother. She was hardly a fit 'carrier' for the antichrist, so out of the window she must go.[95]

That LaVey was a West Coast phenomenon is no accident. Although there were certainly covens in Manhattan, the occultist context for the movie is not really New York but late 1960s California (where all the apartment scenes were filmed). The Californian ambience was likewise cast over independent film-makers: Maya Deren became a Voodoo priestess; Harry Smith was an occultist; Kenneth Anger was a film-maker and Luciferian. Firmly in mainstream Hollywood, those godlike beings, the Hollywood stars were sometimes apt to fall for the allure of the dark arts. Jayne Mansfield visited LaVey after the first public black mass – and has been reported to have been for a short while peripherally involved with Satanists.[96] Jay Sebring, Sharon Tate's old boyfriend, might have gone with Sammy Davis Jr. to a Church of Satan event; thereafter Davis was a sotto voce cheerleader for the movement.[97]

In the 1970s, LaVey suggested that it had become 'fashionable to be a witch', a social position associated with a 'pagan, ecological, and feminist religion'. With its fascination for witches, *Rosemary's*

Baby draws on a sense that the culture is itself in a state of drift, and that cultural symbols and moral values are undergoing a process of renegotiation.[98] The film's lively status as a symbol of transgression, a slow carnivalesque disruption of taboos and norms entwine with that fact. The film bears witness to a revaluation of all values. Here the witch as a cultural figure resides on a strange borderline between what it used to be (the malignant follower of a malevolent prince) and what it is becoming (a symbol of adversarial individualism, connected to a revaluated paganism). Transgression becomes a good in itself. Rosemary stands committed to an older view, and, in the main, the film does too for all that is imbued with the new ideology. Christianity itself is up for revaluation, devalued as weak, debunked and imposed on society. In this way, as in many others, the film seizes a cultural boundary position.

Yet the film lacks any trace of a romantic Satanism. The witches' age perhaps precludes their occultism being a celebration of the body. Rather they represent physicality's limits – decrepitude, loss, and uglification – touching on the long-standing iconography of the elderly witch; the Dionysiac quality of the film's other 'party', the ritual in Rosemary's dream, is decidedly geriatric. Around this time feminists were busy reinventing the sexist image of the crone and hag, returning her to grandmotherly wisdom. Again, the film hardly touches on that: Minnie is a powerful and indomitable figure, but here women follow, men lead, husbands barter and women are raped.

The film – and Rosemary – understand the concept of 'the witch' in various ways. Witches frighten us because they are so hard to detect and delineate. Rosemary defines them in three ways: by their membership of a group, by their involvement in a malign plot, and by their practices. The last of these largely consists of what she imagines or fills in through her researches. Above all, the witch is the enemy, that which is 'not us' – though this distance from us and from our tastes, beliefs and desires is something concealed; part of the horror is that they seem otherwise so like us.[99] They are human and yet linked to a feared, encroaching spirit realm. They are modern figures

committed to a premodern ethos; they are Nietzschean assertors of
the self but also (in their own minds) vestiges of the true 'old religion'.
One lingering early modern idea present in Polanski's film is that it is
the contract that makes the witch. Again, this makes Guy the truest
witch, for it is he who strikes the bargain.

In 1960s countercultural readings, following the Margaret
Murray thesis of a suppressed native pagan religion, the witch was
increasingly understood, historically speaking, as the victim.[100]
In place of this, *Rosemary's Baby* presents the view that they are
doers of harm through malign magic. Magic makes things happen,
and what it produces is vicious (Donald Baumgart's blindness, the
deaths of Mrs Gardenia and Hutch, the summoning of Satan to
rape Rosemary). The witchcraft in *Rosemary's Baby* is not Gerald
Gardner's or Margaret Murray's sequestered religion, it's theatre and
Gothic. Its ambience comes from the 1890s; Satan is not so much the
goat-herd god, as an impresario's conjuration.

According to Sybil Leek, around 1970 there were 300 covens
operating in the USA, though a more conservative estimate puts the
figure at 150.[101] These were secret communities, coteries and cliques
defined by being clandestine. Witches were right for conspiracy
culture because they were popularly understood to be secret and were

indeed in practice enjoined to be so. Like the communist bogeymen of the John Birch Society's imaginings, they were present but hidden. The private and public self fell apart; their selves was the something they had to hide. Yet these covens were not just secret, they were also communal. As sociologist Georg Simmell argued, the secret makes a community, and the community is a secret. Those within the circle protect each other by mutual confidence, by silence in the face of others. They define themselves by what they do not say. Such hiddenness cannot but look sinister; it is both the strength of the group and its weakness. Public exposure might disintegrate it. In *Rosemary's Baby*, the witches are both ideologically private and criminally conspiratorial; what they plan is a rite and a rape.

The planning of that crime itself binds them together. The witches operate through a kind of self-righteousness and also through a kind of guilt. They know that everyone else would believe their plot to be wrong. They stand as a community of transgressors and aggressors, reimagining their own morality within the group. In this way, they present a strong version of 1960s moral relativism; as John Milton's Satan declares, 'evil, be thou my good'.

Nathaniel Hawthorne's 'Young Goodman Brown' or John Buchan's *Witch Wood* (1927) manifest an older version of the trope. There the small community finds its dark double. The fear is of kith and kin, of those you know but find that you do not know. It's an anxiety of the village, repeated in *The Wicker Man*, *Robin Redbreast* and, curiously, *The Stepford Wives*. However, in *Rosemary's Baby*, unless you are a witch, there is no community. Only those in the coven possess this companionship we've otherwise lost. Outside of a dream, we never see any of Rosemary's family; aside from Hutch and her fleeting party guests, no one visits and no one helps. For Guy, there's the acting profession, though that turns out (as far as he's concerned) to be a 'community' dominated by rivalry and ambition. In the absence of a communal frame, Rosemary finds herself adrift between benevolent parental figures (Hutch) and malevolent ones (Dr Sapirstein, Minnie and Roman, and Guy himself). In a world in which loneliness feels customary, the witches help. They are (in some controlling way) 'kind'. Otherwise the city fosters only random friendship groups. Rosemary must have friends, but effectively by a kind of drifting she loses them during the movie. They flit once into her life (they are couples, they are 'their' friends), then vanish.

The movie dramatizes the irritations of urban life, the low-level neighbourly harassment that steals us from ourselves. This fable of American witchcraft entwines with the social conditions of an atomized life and a collapse in neighbourliness. In a lovely premonition of Keith Thomas's 1971 thesis about the origins of witchcraft and the oppressions of neighbourliness, witches are the neighbours who won't leave you alone, those who are too communal, not individualistic enough.

Only fifteen years or so after the Joseph McCarthy 'witch-hunt' and *The Crucible* (1953), *Rosemary's Baby* enacts a persecution, where the persecutors are the witches themselves. Gordon's sinisterly laughable intrusiveness is merely one of the ways in which the movie looks as though it's an off-beat comedy. As one critic noted at the time, the film was not so much about menace, as about annoyance.[102]

Unlike the small community, the city creates randomness. Here that randomness achieves the dark shape of conspiracy. In the arbitrary streets lurks a conspiratorial space. Otherwise the city houses everything, everyone, every kind of perversion, strangeness, belief. (As Dr Hill declares, every kind of crazy person lives in New York.) In this context, the witches' community does not double the mainstream but manifests a splintering of it. In a fragmented zone of beliefs and modes of being, the witches are just one more form of faith, one more 'lifestyle'. In the end, the witches show themselves to be global, a community that crosses borders, Japanese and Greek as much as plain American.

Once they become part of a conspiracy culture, the witches reveal themselves as both weirdly premodern, an ancient survival and highly contemporary. Their 'will to believe' enacts a perverse version of myriad attempts to resacralize the world, though one which, as I have suggested, simultaneously erodes the very idea of the sacred. The violation against sacredness at the centre of the movie is also for the witches an ecstasy, the summoning of their god. As LaVey remarked: 'It's going to take a lot to come up with a film that's as much a blasphemy as *Rosemary's Baby*.'[103]

The film belongs with the millennial atmosphere of its time and the talk of an 'age of Aquarius'. Under the pressure of rapid social change, many were prompted to believe that we were about to enter a new kind of culture and society. Roman's declaration that this is the Year One is symptomatic. A new age requires a new kind of human being. There were beliefs current at the time that the Nazis had been involved in trying to raise or bring to birth a 'new man', a mutant creature that would represent the next evolutionary stage.[104] In this sense – as Vivian Sobchack suggests – the Star Child in *2001, A Space Odyssey* (1968) and Rosemary's baby are siblings.[105] Both signal a new evolutionary stage, a revolutionary threat in the year of revolutions. Both new creatures were also alien creatures, us and not us. One appears benign, the other suggests malignancy; neither yet knows what he will do next.

The will to believe

Let us imagine, once again, that all is only as Rosemary imagines it. In that reading of the film, why would Rosemary choose to believe this fantasy? If the witches don't exist, why make them up? What does Rosemary gain from believing in the witches? In an interview, Polanski demurred at the idea that it was simply to make the world more colourful.[106] Nonetheless, perhaps all the terror in the world finds its compensation in the discovery that we are living within a narrative. The world may be dark, appalling, yet it is still story-shaped, and therefore makes sense.

In the occult interpretation, Rosemary's situation is utterly unique. It may be taken as symptomatic – say, of the medicalization of childbirth or of a crisis in American marriage – but that does nothing to alter its extreme weirdness. She is, as the film insists on, chosen among all women. The story is in aesthetic terms 'interesting'; if it immerses itself in the ordinary, it does so to shatter that category from within. Its shift towards the fantastic, the Gothic, explodes the quotidian world. New York is a place not just of horrors but of supernatural influences.

Rosemary stands, caught between narratives given to her by two men – by Guy, an actor, and by Hutch, an adventure story writer – just the kind of man to invent a Dennis Wheatley-style occult romance: 'Sweet Hutch. He made everything sound like a boy's adventure, didn't he?'[107] In an agnostic world without God, without meaning, the witches really believe in something – and Rosemary too ends up believing in something – even though it is only in witches.

After all that may be preferable to a world in which she is raped by her husband, cut off, bullied, her pregnancy taken away from her. Those things will still be what has happened, but at least they took place on the level of the global (indeed part of a war against heaven) and not as an unnoticed domestic failure. Without the witches, it's a senseless world, where suffering has no meaning. The witches provide that meaning, by being an enemy, and by themselves believing. Rosemary believes too; she fills the emptiness and brutality of her life with a fairy tale, a holy war. Though in the end, as we shall see, something else takes over. If it is a war, she, perhaps, surrenders; if it is a fairy tale, she turns and sides with the witch.

All good things come to an end

What is the *telos* of a Gothic text? Its process is distress, suffering and tension. Its end lies in survival or death, all survivals being only a postponement of mortality. Depending on how you see things, *Rosemary's Baby* ends in acquiescence or otherwise the possibility of love.

Any response to the film's art must conclude, of course, with a discussion of its infamous ending, from the iconic image of Rosemary stalking through the apartment clutching a knife to her final implicit capitulation to command, and to the instincts, choices or social constructions (you decide) involved in motherhood. For a moment, Rosemary herself becomes the object of fear; taking the knife, striding down the corridor, assuming purpose. Earlier, when Rosemary wakes up, she has already scared Laura-Louise. As she gains agency, she gains the capacity to frighten. Yet that brief assumption of power peters out as she walks into the party for her baby.

When Rosemary stalks into the Castevets's apartment, it does now indeed seem to be really happening, and the uncanny reading of the film ought to fall apart. However, some have suggested that even here the camera is by now so entwined with Rosemary's 'psychosis' that we simply see what her illness sees.[108] In this regard, there's an intriguing stage direction in Polanski's script: 'She steps further and further away through the shouting people. In the confusion of movement, a faint fragment of her dream flashes.'[109] It is impossible to say whether this flash of the dream acts as a sign that she now understands it was indeed real or an indication that she's still in her dreaming state.

Either way, the end reaches extremity. Audiences might be genuinely distressed here, really getting, at last, what Gothic is – a form based on the necessity for victimhood, the injustice of the real. The end's tragic loss proffers only the grimmest explanation for events. Instead of evoking an audience's sterile satisfaction at the characters' triumph, the characters (as in all four of Polanski's previous films) are prostrated at the end of the film.[110]

What happens in Rosemary's decision to care for her child proves hard to comprehend. The entire last scene expands into the movie's most uncanny moment, in that we really do seem here to be forced to hesitate between mutually exclusive interpretations. Part of this comes from the film's refusal to grant us any direct view of the baby himself; in absence of certainty, Polanski invites us to imagine. (In a review in the *Evening News*, Felix Barker gives a rather full description of the demonic baby that he has in fact never seen.)[111]

In Anton LaVey's account of the moment, here Rosemary discards her Catholic heritage and discovers her inner Satanist, and achieves triumph in this way, reaching self-realization.[112] Less implausibly, perhaps, the critic F.X. Feeney has seen the moment as invoking a religious feeling, imbued with the awe of a mother's connection to her child – something especially powerful for Polanski, whose mother was so cruelly taken from him.

Minnie seeks to flatter Rosemary that she has been chosen above all women, a mirror-image of the Virgin Mary, perhaps designed to chime with her Catholic education. Certainly, Rosemary agrees to be a mother, to cradle the child. The question is whether this means that the Devil wins the day.[113]

For some, this acquiescence in her role as mother is an appalling capitulation, a submerging of personhood in a constrictive social role. Valerie Solanas's *SCUM Manifesto* had been published in 1967, and Shulamith Firestone's *The Dialectic Of Sex* (1970) was around the corner, both of which represent pregnancy and reproduction as central to the social control of women. Both writers hope for huge decreases in population, even, in Solanas's case, the end of life on earth.

In this reading, here Rosemary joins in the conspiracy against her. Does she give in to evil or to community? Her status as mother is no longer just an event for herself and her child, but for all of them; the Castevets name the baby 'Adrian' and Rosemary's attempts to name it ('Andy or Jenny') fail. Given the strongly hierarchical basis of the witch-society, Adrian is, of course, Roman's father's name. What if Adrian had been Adriana? What if the baby were a girl? The witches assume a patriarchal descent, much as the blasphemous premise of the story requires a son, where Rosemary was content with either possibility, Andy *or* Jenny.

Given the bleakness of the ending here, or in *Repulsion* or *Chinatown*, it may seem perverse to describe Polanski's vision as anything other than a pessimistic one. 'Pessimism,' he has told us, 'in fact, is what life experience teaches us.'[114] Yet in the commentary on *Repulsion*, Polanski insists on his optimism, and I think he's right to do so. The endings often involve defeat, yet there's an inner energy, a brilliance of invention in his films that transforms what might otherwise be negative. Polanski has affirmed: 'Rather, I feel that my escapades, my wildness and strength have sprung from a sense of wonder at what life has to offer.'[115]

Part of the implicit optimism in these last scenes arises from the confusions present in Satan's plan to father a child. On its release, the critic Stuart Byron talked of the theme of the envy of God, that has Satan attempting to reproduce, by parody (he cannot create, only imitate) what God has already done.[116] In 1940, Charles Williams wrote a play offering a preemptive version of *Rosemary's Baby*, in which Satan yearns to become 'incarnate'. God's incarnation as Jesus, the taking of humanity into God, can be understood as redemptive in itself. In that one act, all humanity becomes involved, in the kinship of being here, with God. The ultimate misrule of Christmas appears here: God becomes a human baby. Omnipotence permits its own powerlessness.

The traces of incarnation are the subject of film, a medium that takes the living body, the present person, and transmutes them into the flickering light on a screen. Yet film too longs for the bodies it deposes and displays their traces in figures of revulsion or desire. As we have seen, this movie transmutes the body's urges, to eat, to have sex, the very fertility expressed in pregnancy, into disgust and oppression. A Manichean aversion to the flesh darkens this movie's dispassionate eye.

The film parodies the virgin birth and the incarnation, yet does this ineptly, because Satan is not God, but just 'a god' to the witches, a Zeus, not the very ground of being itself. In any case, the Satan who rapes her is already physical; it is mysterious why such an animalistic figure desires incarnation as a human. It is as though he does not so much wish to descend into humanity, as to rise up to it. As played out in *Rosemary's Baby*, Satan's desire for incarnation evinces an inhuman (and very human) cruelty. It provides an opportunity for a show of power. The Devil's primary aim here may not be the engineering of his birth into the world of humans but simply the degradation of Rosemary. The rape assaults the person in her. Nonetheless the rape, the role of brutal potency and domination, leads to the absolute helplessness of a baby. The infant, their child, now requires Rosemary's powers of nurturance; he is at the mercy of her kindness. The sexual politics of this are more than messy, but we can feel that nurturance really is a good, a returning of care in response to a horrific act of negation. Adrian is powerless, so she helps him. In doing so, it is true that Rosemary remains surrounded by those who still would control and manipulate her, but none of them can make her a mother to the child. That is, perhaps, her choice.

The film may touch upon optimism in a way that would baffle and anger the witches themselves. There is no reason to assume that 'Adrian' will be all evil, or will (in terms of heredity) take after his dad. After all, his mother's goodness is in him too. In Levin's novel, Rosemary considers killing her son, but cannot do so: 'Killing was wrong, no matter what.'[117] This is a thought to which the witches could never attain. Adrian might, after all, be no worse than all of us, mixed in good and evil. He might even be 'good', in spite of his heredity, his conception, the upbringing we might imagine for him. He may have his father's eyes, but why might he not have his mother's heart? He is, after all, equally akin to gentle, courageous, sympathetic Rosemary.

And then comes the film's true end, the return of the overhead shots of the Dakota and the Manhattan streets, with another couple, or perhaps Rosemary and Guy again, as at the beginning, walking into the building. The film becomes circular, returning to its beginning at the end, leaving us with Rosemary's lulling, solitary voice.

The joker in the pack

When, in utter despair, Rosemary drops her kitchen knife into the floor of the Castevets's apartment, Minnie comes forward and plucks it out and rubs the wood with house-proud solicitude. It is the second time in the film that Minnie has worried over the furnishings, the carpet or the parquet. And despite all Rosemary's dire despair, the film is surely here comic.

In *Rosemary's Baby*, Polanski baffles us with an unsettled aesthetic, a movie that may abruptly lunge towards comedy and that at its end resists tragedy, opting instead for the parodic and satiric. Commentators at the time saw a precarious interchangeability of comedy and tragedy as intrinsic to the freedoms of the new Hollywood aesthetic, as present in *Bonnie and Clyde* as in *Rosemary's Baby*.[118] Early in his career, Polanski suggested: 'Everything in life has a comic quality on the surface and a tragic quality underneath'.[119] In *Modern British Dramatists* (1968), John Russell Brown was writing of the 'comedy of menace', a very apt phrase for *Rosemary's Baby*. In many ways, the film is a dreadful practical joke, a derisory trick practised on Rosemary; Polanski, after all, once described himself as 'a mischievous person'.[120]

Interpreting the film as a tragedy might seem to be the proper approach. Certainly there are deaths and the movie can hardly be said to end utterly happily. Gothic perhaps offers violence in the absence of the tragic, oppressing us with suffering without seriousness of affect. There are other indications pushing us in the direction of tragedy: all the actors mentioned by Roman Castevet ('Mrs Fiske and Forbes-Robertson, Otis Skinner and Modjeska') were largely known as tragedians; and, more than anything else, there is the movie's refusal of the possibility of escape. This is a plot with no way out.

Dilys Powell described the press screening of the film in the UK, where while some darkly suspected it was meant to be humorous, not one person cracked a smile.[121] I have attended screenings of the film as solemn. Nonetheless, Polanski was fond of Chaplin, Buster Keaton and Harold Lloyd and these influences bear their impress on *Rosemary's Baby*. The film has its surprising share of comic moments, from Roman's smugly imperturbable conviction that we can name a place and he's been there, to Minnie's strangled cry of 'Carpet!' as the vodka blushes spill, Laura-Louise's spiteful dart of the tongue when she's told to stop rocking Adrian's cradle, or the Greek Satanist's bland inquiry, 'Is this the mother?', and so on. We laugh at those moments, I think, out of irresponsible pleasure, from the release from tension, but above all from an enjoyment of the absurdity of everyday life and ordinary people, their immense capacity to astonish us, including astonishing us by being so typical, so much the type of the nosey neighbour, the suave old man, the downbeat, cardiganed old lady. The incongruity of those types occurring during a Satanic outrage is funny, and more than funny. In this regard, it is curious, but correct, that Rosemary should laugh in the phone booth, struck by the impossible incongruity of her own despair. There are many kinds of laughter. At the film's end, if we do laugh (and at screenings, despite Dilys Powell's experience, many often do), maybe it's because we're asserting on Rosemary's behalf, the joke's power against powerlessness. Otherwise, the joke is simply on Rosemary; the practical jokers reveal their ploy, and so the movie ends.

As we have seen, Polanski has defended the film as 'fun'. *The Fearless Vampire Killers* and *The Ninth Gate* are Gothic, but are indeed suffused with the quality of fun. They are deliciously, spookily light films; in the latter, Emmanuelle Seigner and Johnny Depp engage in a plot that is also a game. Depp says, 'Someone's playing a game with me'; and Seigner replies: 'Of course, you're part of it. And you're getting to like it.' Those films belong to the movie world of boy's adventures, of suspense and mystery. Yet that quality is almost entirely lacking in *Rosemary's Baby*. This may be because it's not an adventure story for a man but a female romance, taking us back to the medieval and early modern world where men go out in to the wild wood and have adventures, while women must be patient and endure. Rosemary is not Sir Gawain, she is Patient Griselda.

Very likely the instability of response in *Rosemary's Baby*, its strange veering from comedy to tragedy, and back again, was a consequence of Polanski's indebtedness to the literature and theatre of the absurd. In 1968, Polanski was saying that absurdism looked out of date and his interest in 'the absurd' was a thing of the past; but such influences are perhaps not so easily shifted.[122] On the Woodhouses' bedside table lies a copy of *The Theatre of Beckett*. (Polanski had long wished to film *Waiting for Godot*, and Beckett had long refused.)[123] Philip Hinchcliffe once wrote: 'I have taken it as axiomatic that for Absurdity to exist, God must be dead.' In that death, 'the world is an existential nightmare from which reason, forgiveness, and hope are absent'.[124] If God is dead, then the film is absurd; if there is still a God (and there might be if there are witches), then it's a conspiracy, and so a kind of a tragedy even – though with hints of a transcendent resolution beyond what the witches plan.

The key critic of the absurd, Martin Esslin declared that the comedy found in the form was produced by the characters' incomprehensibility; the more mysterious and unreadable they are, the more we find them comic.[125] Yet in *Rosemary's Baby*, though perhaps we cannot 'read' her, we do identify with someone, with Rosemary herself. As a result, her fate rarely seems comic to us, connected as we are by empathy and the sharing of her point of view. More, it is Rosemary herself who cannot identify with anyone; other than Hutch and Terry, everyone else is strange to her, and those who are closest are the strangest of all.

Michel Perez has suggested that the outrages in the film were not so much absurd as 'camp'.[126] This is not far-fetched, and Gothic film is often inevitably camp; indeed, the first time the word is said to have appeared in print is in the context of a review of Tod Browning's *Dracula* (1931). Gothic acting is customarily over-the-top, the genre being grounded in deviations from realism, and the people in the film (particularly the witches) migrate from ordinary life to the exaggerated quality of caricature.

The movie possesses the ground between realism and fantasy. In 1966, Polanski had argued that *Repulsion* had shown him how far he could go in the direction of realism.[127] Three years later, after *Cul de Sac* and *Rosemary's Baby*, Polanski declared: 'The more "fantastic" you are, the more realistic you become.' The grotesque proves a path to the real. When asked why Roman Castevet sounds so much like Mister Magoo, Polanski tetchily answers, 'but Mister Magoo *is* a realistic character'.[128]

Perhaps a better term than 'camp' would be that the movie is surreal. In an interview given shortly after the film's release, Polanski confessed that he 'was completely formed by surrealism. Ten years ago, and even at the time I was making my first shorts, I saw everything in the mirror of surrealism.'[129] Yet what really matters in all these foiled attempts at definition is just how far *Rosemary's Baby* unsettles such categories. It is comedy and tragedy; it is grotesque; it is absurd and surreal; it is camp; it is really happening. And it is all these things, unstably, changing from moment to moment, impossible to pin down or label.

3 The Prestige

The reception

On 12 June 1968, the film premiered in New York at the Criterion and Tower East Theatres. Other films released that spring and summer include *2001*, *Planet of the Apes*, *Valley of the Dolls*, *Barbarella*, *The Swimmer*, *Prudence and the Pill*, *The Odd Couple*, *The Green Berets*, and *The Thomas Crown Affair*. It was, in short, a moment for quirky fantasy and strangeness, coming out during the insanity released by Martin Luther King Jr.'s assassination and the shooting of Bobby Kennedy. It was the box office hit of that summer, the summer of the Democratic convention in Chicago, of My Lai, of the Tet Offensive.

Pray for Rosemary's Baby.

At first, Paramount were unsure how to sell the movie. Yet, with a slogan devised by Stephen Frankfurt, Paramount launched a publicity campaign that quickly became an advertising classic.[1] The poster shows Rosemary's reclining face, faded, pallid, and superimposed on it the silhouette of a pram on a rocky landscape. The poster taglines included 'Black magic, exorcism, witchcraft…this shows you where it all began.' But the real classic, the line that perhaps secured the popular success of the film was simply 'Pray for Rosemary's Baby.'

Bad reviews were few. In *Film Quarterly* (perhaps in keeping with that journal's stringent style), Robert Chappetta found it wanting: '*Rosemary's Baby* is a tolerably successful commercial movie, which is to say it isn't very good.'[2] Some found fault with Cassavetes's acting, or more reasonably the possibility that he had been miscast. He was seen as being too 'methody' for the movie's good. There was some faint praise (notably in *The New York Times*, while in *Films and Filming,* Gordon Gow conceded, 'This is a fairly satisfactory film').[3] *Film World* described *Rosemary's Baby*, along with *The Odd Couple* and *Barbarella*, as 'strictly commercial pictures without higher ambitions', in contrast to the artistic endeavour of Zefferelli's *Romeo and Juliet*.[4]

However, not all responses were so tepid. Mostly the film, Polanski and Farrow all garnered high praise, including from the best reviewers of the day – Andrew Sarris and Roger Ebert, Pauline Kael and Penelope Gilliatt, as well as science-fiction writer Harlan Ellison (who could not see any way in which the movie could be bettered).

It won the Donatello Award-Taormina (Director), the Loew's Theatres Inc. Award (Director of the Year), an International Show-A-Rama Award (Director of the Year), a Motion Pictures Arts Club Award (Director), a Motion Picture Exhibitors Award (Ten Top Directors), a Screen Writers Annual Award (Screenplay), an Edgar Allan Poe Special Award (Screenplay), a Nomination for Academy Award (Screenplay), a Foreign Press Nomination for Award (Screenplay), the Best Actress Award for Mia Farrow at the Rio

de Janeiro Film Festival, and a Golden Globe and Best Supporting
Actress Oscar for Ruth Gordon.

The movie's cultural impact was strong and immediate. Soon
Castle was receiving outraged – and threatening – letters, up to fifty
per day.[5] Ray Bradbury wrote: 'I went back to see *Rosemary's Baby*
the other night. I had to go back. I mean, everyone is.'[6]

It was reputed to be the box-office success of the year, and by
early 1969, the film was already reckoned among the top fifty all-time
box-office hits.[7] Paramount were so pleased with the film's success that
they 'negotiated two projects with Polanski for this year and next'.
One was apparently for a film about Paganini and another on the
Donner Pass story, provisionally entitled *The Dinner Party*.[8]

The film's release and its success provided some distraction to
Farrow, who was caught up with the stresses of her divorce. (The
marriage with Sinatra was dissolved in August 1968.[9]) Until that
moment, more commonly regarded as a celebrity, a 'beautiful person',
Rosemary's Baby demonstrated to the world what a formidable actor
she was. Even an antagonistic reviewer such as Chappetta understood
that 'Mia Farrow's performance is the main asset of the film.'[10]

The censorship

To some *Rosemary's Baby's* popularity seemed positive evidence
of society's decline. To these the film was a cynical 'onslaught on
received social morality'.[11] With debatable accuracy, it was declared
to be 'the first U.S.-made major studio film to utilise a four-letter
English vulgarism of debatable justification'.[12] In *The Sunday People*,
discussing the rape scene, Ernest Betts declared, 'No scene I have
encountered in a picture is quite so horrifying as this one. All that stuff
about violence and sex the censor talks about pales beside it.'[13] These
complaints are not purely wrongheaded or specious. It is the business
of this film to make us look at things we might regret having seen.

NCOMP (The National Catholic Office for Motion Pictures)
despised the film, but the question was in 1968 if they still had the
power to break a movie at the box office.[14] This question was quickly

John Trevelyan in the 1960s.

answered in the negative. They condemned seventeen films that year, more than in the previous seven years combined. All flourished, despite (or possibly because of) the ban. (Being condemned was a lucrative marketing device.[15]) In a separate move, the film was reportedly banned in Salem, the haunted home-town of the American witch.[16]

There were more problems in the United Kingdom. In the press, John Trevelyan, Secretary of the British Board of Film Censors, was predicting that 1969 was going to be 'a difficult year for the British Board of Film Censors'; a 'tidal wave of sex obsession' was on its way. In his view, the new 'Rating' procedure would give American film-makers the opportunity to break the 'sex-barrier'. Trevelyan saw the film with Lord Harlech, and decided that it required 15 seconds' worth of cuts. While acknowledging that Polanski was a great director, he felt that the film's 'kinky sex' might encourage support for or interest in the witches, and thereby increase their numbers. Trevelyan is quoted as saying: 'It is not generally known that there is quite a lot of activity of this kind in this country.'[17] With the cut, the film was released as an X.

Polanski, who regarded Trevelyan as a friend, responded by pointing out that the rites were entirely fictional. He rather dramatically suggested the censorship was 'deplorable' and akin to the 'Spanish Inquisition'.[18] The film had its UK premiere at the Paramount Cinema on Lower Regent Street on the evening of Thursday, 25 January 1969. Paramount invited some well-known witches to the premiere, despite the first one they approached demanding £50 for the privilege of attending.[19] That afternoon, Polanski screened the film uncut to an invited London audience. For the theatrical release, those 15 seconds were cut, removing the moments where Rosemary's legs are tied down and Jackie Kennedy incongruously consoles her. Dilys Powell scrutinized the missing 15 seconds and found them 'as explicit and just as idiotic' as the rest of the movie.[20] In the *Morning Star*, Nina Hibbin pointed out that audiences could not see the tying-down but were not spared the rape.[21] As in the USA, the attempt at censorship probably boosted box office returns. In *Kinematograph Weekly*, Graham Clarke suggested that the 'censorship publicity' had given the film a 'flying start' with attracting audiences; it was in any case an 'easily saleable property'.[22]

The curse

When they finished filming the scene where Rosemary confronts the witches, Sidney Blackmer gloomily remarked, 'No good will come of all this "Hail Satan" business.'[23] William Castle came to agree with him, believing the film was cursed.[24] Given Castle's history and character, it's hard to know if this was his last and greatest gimmick; but the evidence suggests it was indeed something he truly believed.

The idea of a cursed film became a recurring myth of the time, attaching itself to *The Omen* (1976) and *The Exorcist* (1973), among others. In his review of the film, Kenneth Tynan wrote: 'This is a thoroughly Manichean movie. For many days after seeing it, one entertains the possibility of being infected by infernal powers.'[25] The demons summoned up in the artifice of those films seemed convincing enough to infect the celluloid itself, to pass through the screen to the viewer. Such fears have a long history, going back to the extra, unaccountable demon dancing among the actors in the original production of Christopher Marlowe's *Doctor Faustus*. Polanski's next film was *Macbeth*, 'the Scottish play', the most famous cursed text of all. When demons are involved, the artwork itself seems apt to grow uncanny.

First, Castle fell ill with uremic poisoning. While he was struggling with the effects of this illness, Komeda too fell seriously ill. After being shoved badly by Marek Hlasko, Polish writer and exile in Los Angeles, and then dropped when Hlasko tried to help him recover, the composer collapsed and fell (like Mrs Gardenia and Hutch) into a coma. After several months he died from hematoma of the brain.

Soon after Castle's recovery, on 8 August 1969, came the incomprehensible devastation of the attack by the Manson Family on Polanski's home on Cielo Drive, and the murder of everyone there, including Jay Sebring, Sharon Tate and her unborn child.

Adding to the grief and horror provoked by the attacks, the press quickly decided that the victims were responsible for their own deaths. There were rumours of drugs, sex orgies, occult rites and ceremonies. Polanski himself came under suspicion, even though he was in London at the time of the murders. Undoubtedly, the media were imagining Polanski and the Cielo Drive killings through the lens of *Rosemary's Baby*. That movie had self-consciously interconnected art and life, even as it ostentatiously insisted on its own artifice, its place as a constructed thing. Now the media were cruelly reversing the game, seeing real people, real deaths, as though they were merely elements in a detective story to be resold to the public.

Polanski understandably believes that Castle's theory is nonsense. Komeda's death and, especially, the Manson Family murders were terrible but belonged to the real world of accident and human wickedness. To put it all down to a 'curse' belittles the suffering, and returns guilt again, as the press were doing anyway, to the film's makers.

Since the murders, Polanski has remained a prominent writer director, with undisputed masterworks such as *Chinatown* (1974), *The Tenant* (1976) and *The Pianist* (2002) still to come. And yet from then on, undoubtedly, something changed in him:

There used to be a tremendous fire within me – an unquenchable confidence that I could master anything if I really set my mind to it. This confidence was badly undermined by the killings and their aftermath. I not only developed a closer physical resemblance to my father after Sharon's death but began to take on some of his traits; his ingrained pessimism, his eternal dissatisfaction with life, his profoundly Judaic sense of guilt, and his conviction that every joyous experience has its price.[26]

It would seem that for much of the 1970s, he fell into a desperate and nihilistic way of life, that would end in 1977 in Los Angeles with him raping a young teenage girl, Samantha Geimer. Following a plea bargain, he admitted that he was guilty of one charge of 'unlawful sexual intercourse with a minor'. In the expectation of ending up with probation, he spent six weeks in state prison undergoing psychiatric evaluation, but afterwards absconded before returning to court for final sentencing, fearing that the judge planned to send him back to prison for years. Since then, Polanski has resided in France, much honoured by the artistic establishment, but unable to return to America where he would most likely face incarceration. Despite Oscars success with *Tess* and *The Pianist*, that horrendous assault on a thirteen-year-old girl necessarily shadows his public image; there are those who regard all his work as polluted by association with him. In relation to this he feels himself misunderstood – in his autobiography, he shows himself disturbingly unable to grasp the cruelty of his act, though more recently he has been in communication with Geimer and has accepted that she was his victim. We see Polanski now through the lens of those ghastly later events, and indeed the events themselves have seemed, as we shall see, an extension of the mood and oppressions of *Rosemary's Baby* itself.

The afterlife

As though the Cielo Drive murders were just another drive-in movie sensation, it was Polanski's appalling fate to see a film about conspiracy absorbed into conspiracy theory. As with the film itself, in the myths around the film coincidences multiply: one of the Manson Family, Susan Atkins, had been a topless dancer for a Church of Satan performance titled 'Topless Witches Review';[27] 'Dear Prudence' from The Beatles' *White Album* was written for Mia Farrow's sister, and that record ended up influencing, perhaps even directing, Charles Manson in his killing spree; in January 1980, John Lennon would be shot in the entrance to the Dakota Building. The film's supposed ties to the Manson

Sharon Tate at a premiere with Polanski.

murders and the killing of Polanski's wife, Sharon Tate, and even to the killing of John Lennon are not necessarily misreadings of the film or even misunderstandings of reality. Rather they show how reality itself, after the film, seems pervaded by the same paranoid, attentive anxieties that lie at its heart. The film expresses, analyses and causes paranoia.

The film influenced many later horror movies, either in expressing the horror of pregnancy, or in drawing on fantasies of the occult and witchcraft. There's word that a porn version, *Rosemary's Beaver* came out soon afterwards (its strapline being 'pray for Rosemary's pussy').[28] John Cassavetes's *Opening Night* (1977) can, at a small stretch, be read as a response to *Rosemary's Baby*, in its use of the uncanny, in its reflections on acting, and with Gena Rowlands's character's desire to change the script echoing Cassavetes's fights with Polanski over improvisation.

The film quickly infiltrated mass culture: the January 1969 issue of *MAD Magazine* had '*Rosemia's Boo-Boo*' on the cover; in early 1969, at performances in Los Angeles of *Hair*, actors carried a placard declaring, 'Nixon is Rosemary's Baby.'[29] The poster became an icon, the movie's plot a shared hallucination for a suspicious American public. Moreover, the movie continues to resonate in the social unconscious: in 2014, NBC produced a Polanski-inflected TV mini-series version of Levin's novel; in the American sitcom, *Parks and Recreation* (2009–2015), Henry Winkler's sinister gynaecologist is called Dr Saperstein. There's a folk band from Nashville called 'All of Them Witches'; there's a French rock group called 'Rosemary's Baby'.[30] Most recently, Quentin Tarantino's *Once Upon a Time in Hollywood* (2019) has woven a glossy revenge fantasy around the Cielo Drive murders; Rafal Zawierucha plays Polanski, and Margot Robbie embodies Sharon Tate.

Although its portrait of witchcraft is hardly celebratory, its most striking influence may be that it abetted the process by which Satanism and the occult became acceptable and trendy. Anton LaVey proposed that:

Rosemary's Baby did for us what *Birth of a Nation* ... did for the Ku Klux Klan ... I never realised what a film could do. I remember reading that at the premiere of D. W. Griffith's *Birth of a Nation* there were recruiting posters for the KKK in southern cities. I chuckled because at the premiere of *Rosemary's Baby*, there were posters of the Church of Satan in the lobby.[31]

The *Sunday Telegraph* imagined the movie as providing a 'Boost for Britain's Witches', or so 'a well-known North London witch' suggested.[32]

    Thirty years after the novel appeared, Levin wrote a sequel, *Son of Rosemary* (1997). Here, at its end, in Alice-in-Wonderland fashion the entire plot of the first novel and film, and its sequel are revealed to be nothing but a dream. Guy and Rosemary lie still in bed, and are yet to move into any new apartment building. It was not real, and none of it was really happening. In any other circumstance, such an ending would truly seem a disenchantment. Yet here, it seems in keeping. For it graces us with a welcome refusal of all the horrors that Rosemary goes through. It keeps her safe. And it returns the story to the place where it always lived, especially on screen, playing before us with the shimmering, troubling insubstantiality of a dream.

Notes

Chapter 1

1 Quoted in Arthur F. McClure, ed., *The Movies: An American Idiom* (Rutherford, NJ: Fairleigh Dickinson University Press, 1971), p. 364.
2 Michel Ciment, Michel Perez, and Roger Tailleur, 'Entretien avec Roman Polanski', *Positif*, no. 102 (February 1969), p. 11.
3 Jack Valenti quoted in 'Young Fans Not All Psychedelic: Valenti', *The Film Daily*, 25 September 1967, p. 3.
4 Michel Perez, 'La petite accouchée de l'amérique', *Positif*, no. 102 (February 1969), p. 1.
5 *Time Magazine*, 21 June 1968.
6 William Castle, *Step Right Up! ... I'm Gonna Scare the Pants off America* (New York: William Castle Productions, 1976), p. 256.
7 Roman Polanski, *Roman* (London: William Heinemann, 1984), p. 227.
8 Castle, *Step Right Up!*, p. 9.
9 Quoted in Ciment, Perez, and Tailleur, 'Entretien avec Roman Polanski', p. 12.
10 'Rosemary's Baby', *Dossiers art et essai*, no. 49 (30 October 1968), p. 17.
11 Simon Crook, 'The Mutant Showman', *Empire*, no. 239 (May 2009), p. 119.
12 Castle, *Step Right Up!*, p. 200.
13 Castle, *Step Right Up!*, p. 201. Did Hitchcock turn down *Rosemary's Baby*? The answer would seem to be that he was never approached, but the rumour persists, as in Julian Jebb, 'Polanski's Devils', *The Listener*, 3 January 1984, p. 35.
14 Robert Evans, *The Kid Stays in the Picture*, revised edition (London: Faber & Faber, 2004), p. 142.

15 Annie Nocenti, 'Adapting and Directing *Rosemary's Baby*', *Scenario*, vol. 5, no. 4 (2001), p. 110.
16 Harrison Engle, 'Polanski in New York', *Film Comment*, vol. 5, no. 1 (Autumn 1968), p. 5; Paul Cronin, ed., *Roman Polanski: Interviews* (Jackson, Mississippi: University of Mississippi Press, 2005), p. 31.
17 Martin Auby and Richard Rayner, 'Roman Scandals', *Time Out*, 19 January 1984, p. 11.
18 'Polanski's Plank', *The Times*, 15 January 1969, p. 8; Thomson, 591.
19 Quoted in Cronin, *Roman Polanski*, p. 114.
20 Quoted in Lawrence Wechsler, 'The Brat's Tale: Roman Polanski', in *Vermeer in Bosnia* (New York: Pantheon, 2004), p. 93.
21 Wechsler, 'The Brat's Tale', p. 103.
22 Quoted in Ciment, Perez, and Tailleur, 'Entretien avec Roman Polanski', p. 14.
23 Cronin, *Roman Polanski*, p. 113.
24 Polanski, *Roman*, p. 228.
25 Nocenti, 'Adapting and Directing', pp. 111, 114.
26 David Robinson, 'Satan in the Suburbs', *Financial Times*, 24 January 1969.
27 Kenneth Tynan, *Observer Review*, 2 February 1969.
28 David Ehrenstein, *Roman Polanski* (Paris: Cahiers du cinema, 2012), p. 20; Edward Z. Epstein and Joe Morella, *Mia: The Life of Mia Farrow* (New York: Delacorte Press, 1991), p. 131.
29 Lee Server, *Ava Gardner* (London: Bloomsbury, 2006), p. 243; Kitty Kelley,

His Way: The Unauthorized Biography of Frank Sinatra (London: Bantam Press, 1986), p. 378. (The latter is, admittedly, a scandal-loving source.)

30 Gordon, 'An Actress in Search of a Character,' pp. 73, 76, quoted in Leslie H. Abrahamson, 'Mia Farrow: Categorically Intangible', in Pamela Robertson Wojcik (ed.), *New Constellations: Movie Stars of the 1960s* (New Brunswick, NJ: Rutgers University Press, 2012), p. 102.

31 Mia Farrow, *Mia Farrow: A Memoir. What Falls Away* (London: Transworld Publishers, 1997), p. 104.

32 Mia Farrow, *Mia Farrow: A Memoir. What Falls Away* (London: Transworld Publishers, 1997), pp. 96, 128.

33 Molly Haskell, *From Reverence to Rape: The Treatment of Women in the Movies*, second edition (Chicago: University of Chicago Press, 1987), p. 346.

34 Pauline Kael, *Deeper Into Movies: The Essential Kael Collection: from '69 to '72* (London: Calder & Boyars, 1975), p. 73.

35 Leslie H. Abrahamson, '"I'm Like A Kaleidoscope": Mia Farrow and the Shifting Prismatics of Modern Femininity in the 1960s', in Su Holmes and Diane Negra (eds.), *In The Limelight and Under the Microscope: Forms and Functions of Female Celebrity* (New York: Continuum, 2011), p. 125.

36 From interview in *Look*, 1 December 1964, quoted in Abrahamson, 'Mia Farrow', p. 93.

37 Abrahamson, 'Mia Farrow', p. 118.

38 Abrahamson, '"I'm Like A Kaleidoscope"', p. 143.

39 Quoted in Nocenti, 'Adapting and Directing', p. 114.

40 Polanski, *Roman*, p. 232.

41 Ray Carney, *Shadows* (London: British Film Institute, 2001), p. 13.

42 Quoted in Ray Carney, ed., *Cassavetes on Cassavetes* (London: Faber & Faber, 2001), pp. 182–184, 247, 183.

43 Polanski, *Roman*, p. 230.

44 Castle, *Step Right Up!*, p. 212.

45 Engle, 'Polanski in New York', p. 5.

46 Richard Sylbert and Sylvia Townsend, *Designing Movies: Portrait of a Hollywood Artist* (Westport, CT: Praeger Publishers, 2006), p. 98.

47 Polanski, *Roman*, 230.

48 Sylbert and Townsend, *Designing Movies*, pp. 98–99.

49 Interview with Richard Sylbert in the DVD 'Retrospective Interviews with Roman Polanski, Robert Evans and Richard Sylbert'.

50 Bob Fisher, 'Dancing With the Devil', *Moviemaker*, vol. 15, no. 76 (Summer 2008), p. 97.

51 Sylbert and Townsend, *Designing Movies*, pp. 99–100.

52 Sylbert and Townsend, *Designing Movies*, p. 104.

53 *The Film Daily*, 2 August, 1967, p. 2.

54 Fisher, 'Dancing With the Devil', p. 97.

55 Engle, 'Polanski in New York', p. 8.

56 As Farrow describes in the 'Conversations' documentary included in the Criterion Collection DVD of *Rosemary's Baby*, produced by Karen Stetler (2012).

57 Farrow, *Mia Farrow*, p. 119.

58 Andrew Sarris, 'The View From New York', *Sight and Sound*, vol. 38, no. 4 (Autumn 1969), p. 203; Alexandre Tylski, *Rosemary's Baby (1968)* (Biarritz: Séguier, 2010), p. 118.

59 Alexander Walker, 'Film Man in Black Magic Row With the Censor', *Evening Standard*, 13 January 1969.

60 Farrow, *Mia Farrow*, p. 121.

61 Engle, 'Polanski in New York', p. 9.

62 Sylbert and Townsend, *Designing Movies*, p. 100; Farrow, *Mia Farrow*, 119–120; Engle, 'Polanski in New York', p. 4.

63 This figure is often quoted by reputable sources; however, a figure of $3.8 million is also cited, similarly from trustworthy sources. I have been unable to determine which is the correct figure.

64 Quoted from a 1971 interview in Cronin, *Roman Polanski*, p. 48; Tylski, *Rosemary's Baby*, p. 95.

65 Polanski, *Roman*, p. 236.

66 Evans, *The Kid Stays in the Picture*, p. 145.

67 Farrow, *Mia Farrow*, p. 123.

68 Polanski, *Roman*, p. 233.

69 Carney, *Cassavetes on Cassavetes*, p. 182.

70 Farrow, *Mia Farrow*, p. 120.

71 Sylbert and Townsend, *Designing Movies*, p. 101.

72 Gabriella Oldham, ed., *John Cassavetes Interviews* (Jackson: University of Mississippi Press, 2016), pp. 16, 41, 85.

73 Ciment, Perez, and Tailleur, 'Entretien avec Roman Polanski', p. 11.

Chapter 2

1 The following synopsis draws in part on the synopsis in the *Rosemary's Baby* press pack.

2 Tylski, *Rosemary's Baby*, p. 44.

3 Komeda's music for the film proved popular. The music was released on a soundtrack LP (No. SLPD 519) on the DOT label by E.M.I. There were also LPs of the music by Stan Kenton on Capitol, the Mertens Brothers on CBS, Doc Severinsen and Strings on the DOT label by E.M.I. and Raymond Leserve and his orchestra on the Major/Minor label – and singles by Mia Farrow, Aris Mardin (both doing 'Lullaby') (Mardin on the Atlantic label) and Claudine Longet doing 'Sleep Safe and Warm' (on PYE).

4 Tylski, *Rosemary's Baby*, pp. 107–108.

5 Ira Levin, *Rosemary's Baby* (1967; London: Corsair, 2011), p. 17.

6 James Morrison, *Roman Polanski* (Urbana: University of Illinois Press, 2007), p. 59.

7 Roman Polanski, *Rosemary's Baby* [Screenplay] (William Castle Enterprises, 24 July 1967), p. 2.

8 Nocenti, 'Adapting and Directing', p. 113.

9 Sylbert and Townsend, *Designing Movies*, p. 102.

10 Quoted in Cronin, *Roman Polanski*, p. 23.

11 Jack Fritscher, *Popular Witchcraft* (Madison: University of Wisconsin Press, 2004), p. 23.

12 Polanski, *Rosemary's Baby*, p. 1.

13 Margaret Tarratt, 'Rosemary's Baby', *Screen*, vol. 10, no. 2 (March/April 1968), p. 92.

14 Levin, *Rosemary's Baby*, p. 14.

15 Levin, *Rosemary's Baby*, pp. 86, 67.

16 Polanski, *Rosemary's Baby*, p. 26.

17 Castle, *Step Right Up!*, p. 211.

18 Castle, *Step Right Up!*, p. 210.

19 From an article in *Esquire*, November 1968.

20 Nocenti, 'Adapting and Directing', p. 114.

21 Polanski, *Roman*, p. 230.

22 Farrow, *Mia Farrow*, pp. 100–101.

23 Thomson, *Biographical Dictionary*, p. 296.

24 Perez, 'La petite accouchée de l'amérique', p. 2.

25 Polanski, *Rosemary's Baby*, pp. 53–54.

26 Leo Litwak, 'Visit to the Town of the Mind', *New York Times*, 4 April 1965, p. 46.

27 Levin, *Rosemary's Baby*, p. 13.

28 Joan Didion, *Slouching Towards Bethlehem* (1968; London: Flamingo, 1993), pp. 122–123.

29 Nocenti, 'Adapting and Directing', p. 114.

30 Nocenti, 'Adapting and Directing', p. 111. Regarding *The Ninth Gate* (1999), Polanski remarked that he would have a hard time making any kind of supernatural film that was not a comedy (Nocenti, 'Adapting and Directing', p. 112). See also Davide Caputo, *Polanski and Perception: The Psychology of Seeing and the Cinema of Roman Polanski* (Bristol: Intellect, 2012), p. 137.

31 Polanski, *Roman*, p. 45.

32 From 'The Moonchild and the Fifth Beatle', *Time*, 7 February 1969, quoted in McClure, *The Movies*, p. 350.

33 Robinson, 'Satan in the Suburbs'; Richard Roud, in *The Guardian*, 26 August 1968.

34 Ciment, Perez, and Tailleur, 'Entretien avec Roman Polanski', p. 9.

35 Polanski quoted in Victor Davis, 'Black Magic – posing a devilish problem for the censor', *Daily Express*, 14 January 1969.

36 Nocenti, 'Adapting and Directing', p. 114.

37 Levin, *Rosemary's Baby*, p. 23.

38 Nocenti, 'Adapting and Directing', p. 111.

39 Venetia Newall, 'The Jew as a Witch Figure', in Venetia Newall (ed.), *The Witch Figure: Folklore Essays by a Group of Scholars in England Honouring the 75th Birthday of Katharine M. Briggs* (London: Routledge & Kegan Paul, 1973), pp. 111–112.

40 Newall, 'The Jew as a Witch Figure', p. 117; Levin, *Rosemary's Baby*, p. 100.

41 'Ce n'est pas mon goût, c'est mon degoût!' (Ciment, Perez, and Tailleur, 'Entretien avec Roman Polanski', p. 16).

42 Nocenti, 'Adapting and Directing', p. 112.

43 Polanski, *Rosemary's Baby*, p. 30.

44 Cronin, *Roman Polanski*, p. 19; Gary Lachman, *Turn Off Your Mind: The Mystic Sixties and the Dark Side of the Age of Aquarius* (New York: Disinformation Company, 2001), pp. 172–175.

45 Morrison, *Roman Polanski*, p. 31.

46 Carol J. Clover, *Men, Women, and Chain Saws: Gender in the Modern Horror Film* (Princeton, NJ: Princeton University Press, 1992), p. 76.

47 Levin, *Rosemary's Baby*, p. 86.

48 Tarratt, 'Rosemary's Baby', pp. 92–93.

49 Polanski, *Rosemary's Baby*, p. 69.

50 Levin, *Rosemary's Baby*, p. 82.

51 Sir Walter Scott, *Minstrelsy of the Scottish Border* (1802–3), vol. 2 (Edinburgh: Oliver and Boyd, 1932), p. 311.

52 Cronin, *Roman Polanski*, p. 29.

53 Quoted from Polanski, and translated from German, in Cronin, *Roman Polanski*, p. 62.

54 Polanski, *Roman*, p. 235.

55 Nocenti, 'Adapting and Directing', p. 111. 'Le récit est semi-subjectif, on est toujours avec elle, mais ce n'est pas son point de vue' (Ciment, Perez, and Tailleur, 'Entretien avec Roman Polanski', p. 12).

56 Polanski, *Roman*, pp. 234–235.

57 Caputo, *Polanski and Perception*, p. 122.

58 Polanski, *Roman*, p. 228.

59 *The Spectator*, 31 January 1969.

60 Polanski, *Roman*, p. 1.

61 Cronin, *Roman Polanski*, p. 17.

62 Nocenti, 'Adapting and Directing', p. 114.

63 Penelope Gilliatt, 'Anguish Under the Skin', *The New Yorker*, 7 June 1968, pp. 87–89.

64 Levin, *Rosemary's Baby*, p. 103.

65 Tylski, *Rosemary's Baby*, p. 100.

66 Levin, *Rosemary's Baby*, pp. 155, 201.

67 Jenny Diski, 'Sitting Inside', *Sight and Sound*, April 1995, p. 13.
68 Fischer, *Popular Witchcraft*, p. 24.
69 Nocenti, 'Adapting and Directing', p. 110.
70 Diski, 'Sitting Inside', p. 12.
71 Nocenti, 'Adapting and Directing', p. 111.
72 See, for instance, 'Par's "Rosemary's Baby" Magic Pic – Magical Bo', in *The Hollywood Reporter*, Wednesday, 29 May 1968, p. 3.
73 Haskell, *From Reverence to Rape*, pp. 346, 347.
74 Diski, 'Sitting Inside', p. 12.
75 Quoted in Cronin, *Roman Polanski*, p. 158.
76 Cronin, *Roman Polanski*, p. 21.
77 Tylski, *Rosemary's Baby*, p. 26.
78 Nocenti, 'Adapting and Directing', p. 192.
79 Polanski, *Rosemary's Baby*, p. 147.
80 Barry Day, 'The Suggestive Experience' [An Interview with Peter Yates], *Films and Filming*, vol. 15, no. 11 (August 1969), p. 7.
81 Polanski, *Rosemary's Baby*, p. 104.
82 Polanski, *Roman*, p. 128.
83 Alexander Walker, 'Not According to Spock ... ', *Evening Standard*, 23 January 1969.
84 Abrahamson, 'Mia Farrow', p. 92.
85 Polanski, *Rosemary's Baby*, p. 130.
86 Polanski, *Rosemary's Baby*, p. 44; Levin, *Rosemary's Baby*, p. 56.
87 Owen Davies, *America Bewitched: The Story of Witchcraft after Salem* (Oxford: Oxford University Press, 2013), p. 203.
88 Beverle Houston and Marsha Kinder, 'Rosemary's Baby', *Sight and Sound*, vol. 38, no. 1 (1968/1969), p. 19.
89 Lucy Fischer, 'Birth Traumas: Medicine, Parturition and Horror in *Rosemary's Baby*', in Graeme Harper and Andrew Moor (eds), *Signs of Life: Medicine & Cinema* (London: Wallflower Press, 2005), p. 21.
90 Sylbert and Townsend, *Designing Movies*, p. 99.
91 Ciment, Perez, and Tailleur, 'Entretien avec Roman Polanski', pp. 8–9.
92 'Polanski's Plank', p. 8.
93 'Polanski's Plank', p. 175.
94 This is an oft-repeated idea, but an informed statement of it can be found in Marcello Truzzi, 'Witchcraft and Satanism', in Edward A. Tiryakian (ed.), *On the Margin of the Visible: Sociology, the Esoteric, and the Occult* (New York: John Wiley & Sons, 1974), p. 216.
95 Fritscher, *Popular Witchcraft*, p. 21.
96 Chris Mathews, *Modern Satanism: Anatomy of a Radical Subculture* (Westport, CT: Praeger, 2009), p. 51.
97 Lachman, *Turn Off Your Mind*, p. 256.
98 Fredrik Gregorius, 'Luciferian Witchcraft: At the Crossroads between Paganism and Satanism', in Per Faxneld and Jesper A. Petersen (eds), *The Devil's Party: Satanism in Modernity* (Oxford: Oxford University Press, 2013), p. 230.
99 See the argument developed in Malcolm Gaskill, *Witchcraft: A Very Short Introduction* (Oxford: Oxford University Press, 2010).
100 See Geoffrey Parrinder, 'The Witch as Victim', in Venetia Newall (ed.), *The Witch Figure: Folklore Essays by a Group of Scholars in England Honouring the 75th Birthday of Katharine M. Briggs* (London: Routledge & Kegan Paul, 1973), pp. 125–138.
101 Truzzi, 'Witchcraft and Satanism', pp. 217–218.
102 Robert Chappetta, 'Rosemary's Baby', *Film Quarterly*, vol. 22, no. 3 (Spring 1969), p. 37.
103 Fritscher, *Popular Witchcraft*, p. 21.

104 Lachman, *Turn Off Your Mind*, pp. 31–37.
105 Vivian Sobchack, 'Child/Alien/Father: Patriarchal Crisis and Generic Exchange', in Constance Penley, Elisabeth Lyon, Lynn Spigel, and Janet Bergstrom (eds), *Close Encounters: Film, Feminism and Science Fiction* (Minneapolis: University of Minnesota Press, 1991), p.3.
106 Ciment, Perez, and Tailleur, 'Entretien avec Roman Polanski', p. 8.
107 Levin, *Rosemary's Baby*, p. 157.
108 Caputo, *Polanski and Perception*, p. 139.
109 Polanski, *Rosemary's Baby*, p. 163.
110 Ciment, Perez, and Tailleur, 'Entretien avec Roman Polanski', p. 17.
111 'What the Devil Do I Make of This?', *Evening News*, 23 January 1969.
112 Fritscher, *Popular Witchcraft*, p. 21.
113 '"Le diable l'emporte"' (Ciment, Perez, and Tailleur, 'Entretien avec Roman Polanski', p. 19).
114 From an interview in 1984, quoted in Cronin, *Roman Polanski*, p. 103.
115 F.X. Feeney, *Roman Polanski*, ed. Paul Duncan (Los Angeles: Taschen, 2006), p. 9.
116 Stuart Byron, '"Rosemary" Poses Fear of Mockery', *Variety*, 19 June 1968.
117 Levin, *Rosemary's Baby*, p. 225.
118 From 'The Shock of Freedom in Films', *Time*, 8 December 1967, quoted in McClure, *The Movies*, pp. 323–325.
119 From an interview in 1963, quoted in Cronin, *Roman Polanski*, p. 5.
120 From the same 1963 interview, in Cronin, *Roman Polanski*, p. 7.
121 '*Rosemary's Baby*', *Sunday Times*, 26 January 1969.
122 Engle, 'Polanski in New York', p. 5.
123 Colin McArthur, 'Polanski', *Sight and Sound*, vol. 38, no. 1 (Winter 1968/1969), pp. 14–15.

124 Arnold P. Hinchcliffe, *The Absurd* (London: Methuen, 1969), pp. vii, 6.
125 Martin Esslin, *The Theatre of the Absurd*, revised edition (New York: Doubleday & Company, 1969), p. 361.
126 Perez, 'La petite accouchée de l'amérique', p. 2.
127 Quoted in Cronin, *Roman Polanski*, p. 9.
128 Quoted in Cronin, *Roman Polanski*, pp. 26, 25.
129 McArthur, 'Polanski', p. 15.

Chapter 3

1 From an interview with Robert Evans, in the 'Conversations' documentary included in the Criterion Collection DVD.
2 Chappetta, '*Rosemary's Baby*', p. 35.
3 Gordon Gow, '*Rosemary's Baby*', *Films and Filming*, vol. 15, no. 6 (March 1969), p. 38.
4 Herbert G. Luft, 'Hollywood Changes Hands', *Film World*, vol. 5, no. 3 (July/September 1969), p. 18.
5 Castle, *Step Right Up!*, p. 229.
6 Ray Bradbury, 'A New Ending to *Rosemary's Baby*', *Films and Filming*, vol. 15, no. 11 (August 1969), p. 10.
7 Perez, 'La petite accouchée de l'amérique', p. 2; 'The Moonchild and the Fifth Beatle', *Time*, 7 February 1969, quoted in McClure, *The Movies*, p. 341.
8 'Paramount, Polanski, Paganini', *Today's Cinema*, 27 January 1969, p. 4; Polanski, *Roman*, pp. 247–248.
9 Farrow, *Mia Farrow*, p. 149.
10 Chappetta, '*Rosemary's Baby*', p. 37.
11 Tarratt, '*Rosemary's Baby*', p. 91.
12 *Variety*, 29 May 1968, p. 6.
13 Ernest Betts, 'A Real Chiller', *The People*, 26 January 1969.
14 Stuart Byron, *Variety*, 19 June 1968.

15 Paul Monaco, *The Sixties* (Berkeley: University of California Press, 2001), p. 56.

16 Ciment, Perez, and Tailleur, 'Entretien avec Roman Polanski', p. 9.

17 From Douglas Marlborough, 'Row Over Mia's Film with the Devil', *Daily Mail*, 14 January 1969.

18 Walker, 'Film Man in Black Magic Row with the Censor'.

19 Davis, 'Black Magic'.

20 Dilys Powell, 'Rosemary's Baby', *Sunday Times*, 26 January 1969.

21 Nina Hibbin, 'You May Disbelieve – but you can still find this disturbing', *Morning Star*, 25 January 1969.

22 Graham Clarke, *Kinematograph Weekly*, 25 January 1969, p. 10.

23 From an interview with Mia Farrow in the 'Conversations' documentary included in the Criterion Collection DVD.

24 Castle, *Step Right Up!*, pp. 231–240.

25 Kenneth Tynan, *Observer Review*, 2 February 1969.

26 Polanski, *Roman*, p. 283.

27 Mathews, *Modern Satanism*, p. 53.

28 'Priez pour le chat de Rosemary' (Ciment, Perez, and Tailleur, 'Entretien avec Roman Polanski', p. 11).

29 Michael Billington, 'The Theatre in Los Angeles', *The Times*, 25 January 1969, p. 21.

30 Tylski, *Rosemary's Baby*, p. 81.

31 Quoted in Fritscher, *Popular Witchcraft*, p. 20.

32 'Boost for Britain's Witches', *Sunday Telegraph*, 19 January 1969.

Credits

Rosemary's Baby
USA/1968

Directed by
Roman Polanski
Produced by
William Castle
Associate Producer
Dona Holloway
Screenplay by
Roman Polanski,
based on the novel by
Ira Levin
Cinematography by
William A. Fraker

© 1968. Paramount
Pictures Corporation
and William Castle
Enterprises Inc.
Production Companies
Paramount Pictures
Corporation and William
Castle Enterprises Inc.
Studio
Paramount Pictures
Corporation

Assistant Director
Daniel McCauley
**Second Assistant
Director**
Gene Marum
**Production
Management**
William Davidson
Camera Operator
Michael P. Joyce
Lighting Technician
Steve Birtles

**Special Stills
Photographer**
Robert Willoughby
**Visual Effects/Process
Photography**
Farciot Edouart
Edited by
Sam O'Steen
Bob Wyman
Production Designer
Richard Sylbert
Art Direction
Joel Schiller
Set Decoration
Robert Nelson
**Wig Designer/
Hairstyles Creator for
Mia Farrow**
Sydney Guilaroff
**Hairstylist for Mia
Farrow**
Vidal Sassoon
Make-up
Allan Snyder
Hair Stylist
Sherry Wilson
Costume Design by
Anthea Sylbert
Sound Recordist
Harold Lewis
Dialogue Coach
Hawk Koch (as Howard
W. Koch)
Script Continuity
Luanna Poole
**Body Double for Mia
Farrow**
Linda Brewerton

Music by
Krzystof Komeda (as
Christopher Komeda)
Ludwig van Beethoven,
'Für Elise'
**Title Song, 'Lullaby',
Sung by**
Mia Farrow

CAST
Mia Farrow
Rosemary Woodhouse
John Cassavetes
Guy Woodhouse
Ruth Gordon
Minnie Castevet
Sidney Blackmer
Roman Castevet (Steven
Marcato)
Maurice Evans
'Hutch' (Edward
Hutchins)
Ralph Bellamy
Dr Sapirstein
**Victoria Vetri (as Angela
Dorian)**
Terry Gionoffrio
Patsy Kelly
Laura-Louise
Elisha Cook
Mr Nicklas
Charles Grodin
Dr Hill
**Hanna Hertelendy (as
Hanna Landy)**
Grace Cardiff
Philip Leeds
Dr Shand
D'Urville Martin
Diego

Hope Summers
Mrs Gilmore
Emmaline Henry
Elise Dunstan
(Rosemary's Girlfriend
at Party)
Marianne Gordon
Joan Jellicoe (Rosemary's
Girlfriend at Party)
**Wendy Wagner (Wende
Wagner)**
Tiger (Rosemary's
Girlfriend at Party)
Jack Knight
Policeman Investigating
Terry's Suicide

Walter Baldwin
Mr Wees
Lynn Brinker
Sister Veronica
Jean Inness
Sister Agnes
Patricia Ann Conway
Jacqueline Kennedy
Paul Denton
Skipper/John F. Kennedy
Michael Shillo
The Pope
Clay Tanner
The Devil
Marilyn Harvey
Dr Sapirstein's
Receptionist

Sebastian Brook
Argyron Stavropolous
Ernest Harada
Young Japanese Man
Tony Curtis
Donald Baumgart
William Castle
Man Outside Phone Booth

Premiered in New York
on 12 June 1968.
Premiered in London
on 25 January 1969.
Running time: 137
minutes.
12 290 feet.

Bibliography and Further Reading

Abrahamson, Leslie H. '"I'm Like A Kaleidoscope": Mia Farrow and the Shifting Prismatics of Modern Femininity in the 1960s', in Su Holmes and Diane Negra (eds), *In The Limelight and Under the Microscope: Forms and Functions of Female Celebrity* (New York: Continuum, 2011), pp. 125–148.

Abrahamson, Leslie H. 'Mia Farrow: Categorically Intangible', in Pamela Robertson Wojcik (ed.), *New Constellations: Movie Stars of the 1960s* (New Brunswick, NJ: Rutgers University Press, 2012), pp. 91–114.

Armstrong, Michael. 'On Violence', *Films and Filming*, vol. 15, no. 6 (March 1969), pp. 20–31.

Auby, Martin and Richard Rayner. 'Roman Scandals', *Time Out*, 19 January 1984, pp. 11–14.

Betts, Ernest. 'A Real Chiller', *The People*, 26 January 1969.

Billington, Michael. 'The Theatre in Los Angeles', *The Times*, 25 January 1969, p. 21.

Bradbury, Ray. 'A New Ending to *Rosemary's Baby*', *Films and Filming*, vol. 15, no. 11 (August 1969), pp. 4–9.

Byron, Stuart. '"Rosemary" Poses Fear of Mockery', *Variety*, 19 June 1968.

Caputo, Davide. *Polanski and Perception: The Psychology of Seeing and the Cinema of Roman Polanski* (Bristol: Intellect, 2012).

Carney, Ray. *Shadows* (London: British Film Institute, 2001).

Carney, Ray, ed. *Cassavetes on Cassavetes* (London: Faber & Faber, 2001).

Castle, William. *Step Right Up! … I'm Gonna Scare the Pants off America* (New York: William Castle Productions, 1976).

Chapetta, Robert. '*Rosemary's Baby*', *Film Quarterly*, vol. 22, no. 3 (Spring 1969), pp. 35–38.

Christie, Ian. '*Rosemary's Baby*', *Monthly Film Bulletin*, vol. 38, no. 425 (May 1969), pp. 95–96.

Ciment, Michel, Michel Perez and Roger Tailleur. 'Entretien avec Roman Polanski', *Positif*, no. 102 (February 1969), pp. 6–19.

Clarke, Graham. '*Rosemary's Baby*', *Kinematograph Weekly*, 25 January 1969, p. 10.

Clover, Carol J. *Men, Women, and Chain Saws: Gender in the Modern Horror Film* (Princeton, NJ: Princeton University Press, 1992).

Cronin, Paul, ed. *Roman Polanski: Interviews* (Jackson: University of Mississippi Press, 2005).

Crook, Simon. 'The Mutant Showman', *Empire*, no. 239 (May 2009), pp. 118–123.

Davies, Owen. *America Bewitched: The Story of Witchcraft after Salem* (Oxford: Oxford University Press, 2013).

Davis, Victor. 'Black Magic – Posing a Devilish Problem for the Censor', *Daily Express*, 14 January 1969.

Day, Barry. 'The Suggestive Experience' [An Interview with Peter Yates], *Films and Filming*, vol. 15, no. 11 (August 1969), pp. 4–9.

Delahaye, Michael and Jean-André Fieschi. 'Landscape of a Mind', [An Interview with Roman Polanski from *Cahiers du Cinema*, no. 3, February 1966], in Roman Polanski,

Three Film Scripts: Knife in the Water, Repulsion *and* Cul-De-Sac (London: Lorrimer Publishing, 1975), pp. 205–214.

Didion, Joan. *Slouching Towards Bethlehem* (1968; London: Flamingo, 1993).

Diski, Jenny. 'Sitting Inside', *Sight and Sound,* April 1995, pp. 12–13.

Ehrenstein, David. *Roman Polanski* (Paris: Cahiers du cinema, 2012).

Engle, Harrison. 'Polanski in New York', *Film Comment,* vol. 5, no. 1 (Autumn 1968), pp. 4–11.

Epstein, Edward Z. and Joe Morella. *Mia: The Life of Mia Farrow* (New York: Delacorte Press, 1991).

Esslin, Martin. *The Theatre of the Absurd,* revised edition (New York: Doubleday & Company, 1969).

Evans, Robert. *The Kid Stays in the Picture,* revised edition (London: Faber & Faber, 2004).

Eyles, Allen. '*Dance of the Vampires*', *Films and Filming,* vol. 15, no. 4 (January 1969), p. 40.

Farrow, Mia. *Mia Farrow: A Memoir. What Falls Away* (London: Transworld Publishers, 1997).

Faxneld, Per and Jesper A. Petersen, eds. *The Devil's Party: Satanism in Modernity* (Oxford: Oxford University Press, 2013).

Feeney, F.X. *Roman Polanski,* ed. Paul Duncan (Los Angeles: Taschen, 2006).

Fischer, Lucy. 'Birth Traumas: Medicine, Parturition and Horror in *Rosemary's Baby*', in Graeme Harper and Andrew Moor (eds), *Signs of Life: Medicine & Cinema* (London: Wallflower Press, 2005), pp. 19–32.

Fisher, Bob. 'Dancing With the Devil', *Moviemaker,* vol. 15, no. 76 (Summer 2008), pp. 96–98.

Fritscher, Jack. *Popular Witchcraft* (Madison: University of Wisconsin Press, 2004).

Fry, Carrol L. *Cinema of the Occult: New Age, Satanism, Wicca, and Spiritualism in Film* (Bethlehem, PA: Lehigh University Press, 2008).

Gallagher, Eugene V. 'Sources, Sects and Scripture: The Book of Satan in *The Satanic Bible*', in Per Faxneld and Jesper A. Petersen (eds), *The Devil's Party: Satanism in Modernity* (Oxford: Oxford University Press, 2013), pp. 103–122.

Gaskill, Malcolm. *Witchcraft: A Very Short Introduction* (Oxford: Oxford University Press, 2010).

Gilliatt, Penelope. 'Anguish Under the Skin', *The New Yorker,* 7 June 1968, pp. 87–89.

Gow, Gordon. '*Rosemary's Baby*', *Films and Filming,* vol. 15, no. 6 (March 1969), pp. 38–39.

Greenberg, James. *Roman Polanski: A Retrospective* (Bath: Palazzo Editions, 2013).

Gregorius, Fredrik. 'Luciferian Witchcraft: At the Crossroads between Paganism and Satanism', in Per Faxneld and Jesper A. Petersen (eds), *The Devil's Party: Satanism in Modernity* (Oxford: Oxford University Press, 2013), pp. 229–249.

Haskell, Molly. *From Reverence to Rape: The Treatment of Women in the Movies,* second edition (Chicago: University of Chicago Press, 1987).

Hibbin, Nina. 'You May Disbelieve – but you can still find this disturbing', *Morning Star,* 25 January 1969.

Hinchcliffe, Arnold P. *The Absurd* (London: Methuen, 1969).

Houston, Beverle and Marsha Kinder. '*Rosemary's Baby*', *Sight and Sound,* vol. 38, no. 1 (1968/1969), pp. 17–19.

Jebb, Julian. 'Polanski's Devils', *The Listener*, 3 January 1984, p. 35.

Kael, Pauline. *Deeper Into Movies: The Essential Kael Collection: from '69 to '72* (London: Calder & Boyars, 1975).

Kael, Pauline. *Going Steady: Film Writings 1968–1969* (New York: Marion Boyars, 2000).

Keech, Andrew. '*Rosemary's Baby*', *Music From the Movies* (Leeds: Music From the Movies, 2005), p. 71.

Kelley, Kitty. *His Way: The Unauthorized Biography of Frank Sinatra* (London: Bantam Press, 1986).

Komeda: A Soundtrack for a Life [Film], Dir.Claudia Butenhoff-Duffy (Germany/Poland/Switzerland/ Finland: Benedikt Pictures, Studio Filmowe Kalejdoskop, and ZDF/ Arte, 2010).

Lachman, Gary. *Turn Off Your Mind: The Mystic Sixties and the Dark Side of the Age of Aquarius* (New York: Disinformation Company, 2001).

LaVey, Anton. *The Satanic Rituals* (New York: Avon Books, 1972).

Levin, Ira. *Rosemary's Baby* (1967; London: Corsair, 2011).

Litwak, Leo. 'Visit to the Town of the Mind', *New York Times*, 4 April 1965, p. 46.

Luft, Herbert G. 'Hollywood Changes Hands', *Film World*, vol. 5, no. 3 (July/ September 1969), pp. 17–19.

Madsen, Axel. '"Below the Belt" Cinema', *Film World*, vol. 5, no. 3 (July/ Sept 1969), pp. 15–16.

Marlborough, Douglas. 'Row Over Mia's Film with the Devil', *Daily Mail*, 14 January 1969.

Mathews, Chris. *Modern Satanism: Anatomy of a Radical Subculture* (Westport, CT: Praeger, 2009).

McArthur, Colin. 'Polanski', *Sight and Sound*, vol. 38, no. 1 (Winter 1968/1969), pp. 14–17.

McClure, Arthur F., ed. *The Movies: An American Idiom* (Rutherford, NJ: Fairleigh Dickinson University Press, 1971).

Mia and Roman [Film], Dir. Hatami (country, 1968).

Monaco, Paul. *The Sixties* (Berkeley: University of California Press, 2001).

Morrison, James. *Roman Polanski* (Urbana: University of Illinois Press, 2007).

Newall, Venetia. 'The Jew as a Witch Figure', in Venetia Newall (ed.), *The Witch Figure: Folklore Essays by a Group of Scholars in England Honouring the 75th Birthday of Katharine M. Briggs* (London: Routledge & Kegan Paul, 1973), pp. 95–124.

Nocenti, Annie. 'Adapting and Directing *Rosemary's Baby*', *Scenario*, vol. 5, no. 4 (2001), pp. 108–115, 192.

Oldham, Gabriella, ed. *John Cassavetes Interviews* (Jackson: University of Mississippi Press, 2016).

Parrinder, Geoffrey. 'The Witch as Victim', in Venetia Newall (ed.), *The Witch Figure: Folklore Essays by a Group of Scholars in England Honouring the 75th Birthday of Katharine M. Briggs* (London: Routledge & Kegan Paul, 1973), pp. 125–138.

'Par's "Rosemary's Baby" Magic Pic – Magical Bo', *The Hollywood Reporter*, Wednesday, 29 May 1968, p. 3.

Perez, Michel. 'La petite accouchée de l'amérique', *Positif*, no. 102 (February 1969), pp. 1–5.

'Polanski's Plank', *The Times*, 15 January 1969, p. 8.

Polanski, Roman. *Roman* (London: William Heinemann, 1984).

Polanski, Roman. *Rosemary's Baby* [Screenplay] (William Castle Enterprises, 24 July 1967).

Polanski, Roman. *Three Film Scripts: Knife in the Water, Repulsion and Cul-De-Sac* (London: Lorrimer Publishing, 1975).

Powell, Dilys. 'Rosemary's Baby', *Sunday Times*, 26 January 1969.

Robinson, David. 'Satan in the Suburbs', *Financial Times*, 24 January 1969.

'Rosemary's Baby', *Dossiers art et essai*, No. 49 (30 October 1968), pp. 15–18.

Rosemary's Baby [DVD], 'Conversations', produced by Karen Stetler (Criterion Collection, 2012).

Sarris, Andrew. 'The View From New York', *Sight and Sound*, vol. 38, no. 4 (Autumn 1969), pp. 202–203.

Scott, Sir Walter. *Minstrelsy of the Scottish Border* (1802–3), 4 vols. (Edinburgh: Oliver and Boyd, 1932).

Server, Lee. *Ava Gardner* (London: Bloomsbury, 2006).

Sobchack, Vivian. 'Child/Alien/Father: Patriarchal Crisis and Generic Exchange', in Constance Penley, Elisabeth Lyon, Lynn Spigel, and Janet Bergstrom (eds), *Close Encounters: Film, Feminism and Science Fiction* (Minneapolis: University of Minnesota Press, 1991), p. 3–32.

Sylbert, Richard and Sylvia Townsend. *Designing Movies: Portrait of a Hollywood Artist* (Westport, CT: Praeger Publishers, 2006).

Tarratt, Margaret. 'Rosemary's Baby', *Screen*, vol. 10, no. 2 (March/April 1968), pp. 90–95.

Taylor, John Russell. 'A Glossy Psychological Thriller', *The Times* (23 January 1969).

Thompson, David. '"I Make Films For Adults"' [Interview with Roman Polanski], *Sight and Sound*, April 1995, pp. 6–11.

Thomson, David. *A Biographical Dictionary of Film*, revised edition (London: Andre Deutsch, 1994).

Trevelyan, John. 'Breaking the Sex Barrier', *Today's Cinema*, 15 January 1969, p. 5.

Truzzi, Marcello. 'Witchcraft and Satanism', in Edward A. Tiryakian (ed.), *On the Margin of the Visible: Sociology, the Esoteric, and the Occult* (New York: John Wiley & Sons, 1974), pp. 215–222.

Tylski, Alexandre. *Rosemary's Baby (1968)* (Biarritz: Séguier, 2010).

Tynan, Kenneth. 'Rosemary's Baby', *Observer Review*, 2 February 1969.

Walker, Alexander. 'Film Man in Black Magic Row with the Censor', *Evening Standard*, 13 January 1969.

Walker, Alexander. 'Not According to Spock ...', *Evening Standard*, 23 January 1969.

Wechsler, Lawrence. 'The Brat's Tale: Roman Polanski', in *Vermeer in Bosnia* (New York: Pantheon, 2004), pp. 83–150.

'What the Devil Do I Make of This?', *Evening News*, 23 January 1969.

'Young Fans Not All Psychedelic: Valenti', in *The Film Daily*, 25 September 1967, p. 3.